CONTENTS

||||| KT-158-972 ||||||||||||||||||||||||||||||||

Clockwise from top: Þingvellir National Park; Seljalandsfoss; Gló; whale watching boat in Reykjavík harbour; cyclists on Laugavegur

REYKJAVÍK

If you're more used to the traffic-clogged streets of other major European cities, Reykjavík's sense of space and calm will come as a breath of fresh air. That said, the world's most northerly capital still dwarfs Iceland's other built-up areas, with the Greater Reykjavík area home to two out of every three Icelanders. The atmosphere generated by this bustling port, with its highbrow museums, colourful streets and buzzing nightlife, has earned the city a reputation for hedonistic revelry which draws visitors from across the globe, in record-breaking numbers – and its popularity shows no signs of waning.

Hallgrímskirkja

The Northern Lights over Reykjavík Harbour

Split roughly into two halves by the brilliant waters of Tjörnin lake, the tiny city centre is more a place to amble around and take in the suburban-looking streets and corner cafés than somewhere to hurtle about, ticking off attractions. Reykjavík lacks the grand and imposing buildings found in other Nordic capitals, possessing instead apparently ramshackle clusters of houses, either clad in garishly painted corrugated iron or daubed in pebbledash as protection against the ferocious North Atlantic storms. This rather unkempt feel, though, is as much part of the city's charm as the views across the sea to glaciers and the sheer mountains that form the backdrop to the streets. Even in the heart of this capital, nature is always in evidence – there can be few other cities in the world, for example, where greylag geese

When to visit

Icelandic weather is notoriously unpredictable. In summer, Reykjavík tends to be cloudy and showery, though there can be long, clear spells of sunny weather, too. However, one thing is consistent – it's never really warm. Summer in Reykjavík is more about the long daylight hours than a sudden surge in temperature – the average summer range in the city is 8–14°C. Since Reykjavík lies south of the Arctic Circle, it doesn't experience true Midnight Sun, though nights are light from mid-May to early August. Conversely, in winter, days are short and dark – at the shortest time of the year, in December, the sun doesn't rise until around 10.30–11am, setting again just a couple of hours later. Between September and January, there's a good chance of seeing the Northern Lights. During winter, storms are frequent and temperatures tend to hover a few degrees either side of freezing point.

regularly overfly the busy centre, sending bemused visitors, more accustomed to pigeons, scurrying for cover.

In the midst of the essentially residential city centre, it is the Hallgrímskirkja, a gargantuan white concrete church towering over the surrounding houses, that is the most enduring image of Reykjavík. Below this, the elegant shops and stylish bars and restaurants that line the main street and commercial thoroughfare of Laugavegur are a consumer's heaven. The central core of streets around Laugavegur and Skólavörðustígur is where you'll find a range of engaging museums, too. The displays in the Landnámssýning and the Saga Museum, for example, offer an accessible introduction to Iceland's stirring past; while whale-watching and puffin-spotting tours from

the city harbour give you a chance to experience Icelandic nature up close.

If you have some time to spare, it's well worth venturing outside the city limits to explore some of southwest Iceland's greatest attractions. Top of everyone's list is the erupting geyser known as Strokkur, plus the nearby rift valley, Þingvellir, where you can see a clear split in the earth's tectonic plates; both are easily accessible on day-trips from the capital. A little further afield, the Westman Islands, scene of the famous 1973 volcanic eruption, beckon enticingly, while the rugged natural beauty of Þorsmörk national park and the Landmannalaugar geothermal springs – which mark the jumping-off point into Iceland's remote and uninhabited Interior – are equally worthy of your time.

Best places to swim

Reykjavík has several excellent swimming pools to choose from. The biggest is Laugardalslaug, with outdoor pools and hot pots (see p.71). Following extension work in 2017, Sundhöllin (see p.125) now boasts a large new outdoor pool, in addition to its exisiting indoor one. It also has hot pots and sun terraces. Most visitors can't wait to try the geothermal hot pots and sea lagoon at Nauthólsvík, where there's also a glorious sandy beach (see p.68). Wherever you swim, you must shower thoroughly without a swimming costume before entering the water, since it is not treated with chlorine.

Laugardalslaug

Where to...

Shop

Reykjavík's main thoroughfare, Laugavegur, and the Kringlan shopping centre are where you'll find most of the city's **shops**. That said, Skólavörðustígur is beginning to ramp up its act and now comes a close second to Laugavegur. Remember that most goods are available at tax-free prices when exported from Iceland – ask in store when browsing for details of the cash refund you're entitled to (see p.129). Particularly good-value purchases include anything made of **wool** – from traditional sweaters, gloves and scarves to blankets, shawls and hats.

OUR FAVOURITES: Kolaportið p.37. **Iða** p.50. **Víkurprjón** p.101.

Eat

The one thing every visitor remembers about a visit to Reykjavík is eating the freshest **fish** they have ever tasted. In fact, there are many Icelanders who simply refuse to order fish when they travel abroad, because it doesn't taste like it does at home. In recent years there's been a veritable explosion in the number of fish restaurants in Reykjavík, serving unusual options such as catfish and blue ling alongside more common species like cod and haddock. The other Icelandic staple is mountain **lamb**, which is as succulent as you would expect, and available in most restaurants. Look out for lunchtime specials (often set menus) when prices are much lower than in the evening.

OUR FAVOURITES: Einar Ben p.30. **Lækjarbrekka** p.58. **Fjörubuðið** p.101.

Drink

Drinking in Reykjavík is expensive. However, there are several ways to cut costs. Consider buying wine, beer or spirits on arrival, at the duty-free store inside Keflavík airport. Ask the helpful staff about your duty-free allowances. Alternatively, buy your booze from the **state-run alcohol stores**, *vínbúðin* (see p.30 & p.74), dotted across the city, where prices are higher than at duty free but less than in bars and restaurants. Of course, having a drink in a bar is also tempting – to cut costs, look out for happy hours when prices on alcohol are slashed. Drinking with food in a café or restaurant, though, can soon add up.

OUR FAVOURITES: Micro Bar p.31. **SKÝ Lounge & Bar** p.45. **Bravó** p.59.

Go out

Reykjavík is deservedly known for its **nightlife**. Although the scene is actually no bigger than that of any small-sized town in most other countries, what sets it apart is the northerly setting and location for all this revelry – during summer, it's very disorientating to have entered a nightclub in the wee small hours with the sun just about to set, only to emerge a couple of hours later into the blinding and unflattering daylight of the Icelandic morning. The **bars and clubs** of Austurstræti, Hafnarstræti and Laugavegur are likely to be where you'll spend your time. It can be fun to join in when clubbers spill out into Lækjartorg early on Saturday and Sunday mornings for an alfresco end to the night.

OUR FAVOURITES: Tivoli p.39. **Gaukurinn** p.39. **Hverfisbarinn** p.59.

Reykjavík at a glance

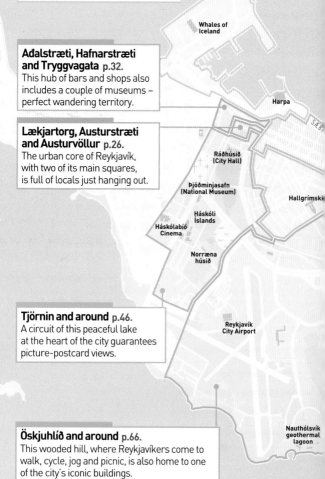

The harbour p.40.
Busy with fishing trawlers and
whaling ships, the harbour area
boasts some fine cultural venues, too.

**Aðalstræti, Hafnarstræti
and Tryggvagata** p.32.
This hub of bars and shops also
includes a couple of museums –
perfect wandering territory.

**Lækjartorg, Austurstræti
and Austurvöllur** p.26.
The urban core of Reykjavík,
with two of its main squares,
is full of locals just hanging out.

Tjörnin and around p.46.
A circuit of this peaceful lake
at the heart of the city guarantees
picture-postcard views.

Öskjuhlíð and around p.66.
This wooded hill, where Reykjavíkers come to
walk, cycle, jog and picnic, is also home to one
of the city's iconic buildings.

Whales of
Iceland

Harpa

Ráðhúsið
(City Hall)

Þjóðminjasafn
(National Museum)

Hallgrímski

Háskóli
Íslands

Háskólabíó
Cinema

Norræna
húsið

Reykjavík
City Airport

Nauthólsvík
geothermal
lagoon

KÓPAVOGUR

Viðey

Bankastræti and around p.52.
Home to Reykjavík's main commercial artery and a number of fine historical buildings.

Hallgrímskirkja and around p.60.
The city's landmark building is a modernist triumph – and there are other sculptural highlights in the area, too.

Viðey Ferry Terminal

Sigurjón Ólafsson Museum

SÆBRAUT

SÆBRAUT

Höfði

Laugardalslaug

Laugardalsvöllur

Ásmundursafn

Botanical Garden

Laugardalshöll

Húsdýragarðurinn

Kjarvalsstaðir

MÚLINN

Fjölskyldu-garðurinn

MIKLABRAUT

Kringlan shopping centre

MIKLABRAUT

rlan

City Theatre

Eastern Reykjavík p.70.
A sporty corner of town, with its largest sports stadium and principal swimming pool.

Things not to miss

It's not possible to see everything that Reykjavík has to offer in one trip – and we don't suggest you try. What follows is a selective taste of the city's highlights, from engaging museums to jaw-dropping landscapes.

∧ **Landmannalaugar**
p.106
The quintessential Icelandic experience – bathing in a geothermal hot spring amid wilderness landscapes which ooze rugged grandeur.

< **The view from Hallgrímskirkja tower**
p.60
The classic view of Reykjavík, with the city's multicoloured buildings laid out below you.

> **Seljalandsfoss**
p.96
Paths run behind the curtain of water at these falls, giving a breathtaking perspective.

< Þingvellir
p.86
See the rift valley where the Eurasian and North American tectonic plates are literally tearing apart.

> Glacier tours
p.125
They don't come cheap, but a trip to, onto and even into an Icelandic glacier is unforgettable.

> Gullfoss
p.90
One of the most popular tourist attractions in Iceland, the Hvítá cascades down a three-step staircase before plunging, in two more stages, into a deep crevice.

< **Harpa**
p.42
Unsurpassed views of the harbour area unfold from the top floor of the city's opera house.

∨ **Þjóðminjasafn**
p.48
The examples of medieval church art inside the National Museum are some of Iceland's finest treasures.

< Strokkur
p.90
The erupting geyser that
everyone wants to see
– Strokkur shoots a spout
of boiling water 30m into
the air every few minutes.

> Whale watching
p.43
Regular boat tours depart
from the city harbour to
spot whales throughout
the year.

< Blue Lagoon
p.80
Lolling around in the geothermal, silica-rich waters here is not just relaxing – it's also extremely good for your skin.

∨ Saga Museum
p.40
At Reykjavík's answer to Madame Tussauds, come face to face with the main characters of the Sagas – and even sample the smells of the Viking period.

< **Horseriding**
p.126
With their fifth gait – a cross between a trot and a canter, called *tölt* – riding an Icelandic horse is a unique experience.

> **Landnámssýning**
p.32
Discover how Reykjavík's first settlers lived and see the extensive remains of a tenth-century Viking hall.

> **Nauthólsvík**
p.68
Bathe in the sublime waters of Nauthólsvík geothermal lagoon and hot pots for free.

< **Skógarfoss**
p.98
A drop of over 60m makes
this waterfall one of the most
impressive in southern Iceland
– particularly when viewed from
the river bed.

∨ **Laugardalslaug**
p.71
Iceland's biggest and best
swimming pool. There's a 50m
outdoor pool, plus smaller
children's pools, as well as
several hot pots.

Day one in Reykjavík

Whales of Iceland p.42. Begin the day checking out the life-size, silicone models of the whales found in Icelandic waters and learn all about these giants of the sea.

Whale watching p.43. Head down to the harbour and go in search of the real thing – humpback whales are the most likely to show – on a whale-watching tour off the Reykjavík coast.

Whales of Iceland

Lunch p.30. An easy walk from the harbour, *Apótek* serves a good-value fishy lunch, amid a beautifully appointed interior.

Þjóðminjasafn p.48. Get to grips with Iceland's stirring past at the National Museum, whose exhibitions on Viking graves, medieval church art and DNA testing are first class.

Tjörnin p.46. From the National Museum, take a pleasant stroll back into the city centre along the banks of Tjörnin lake, for some great views of Reykjavík and its birdlife.

Hallgrímskirkja p.60. Ride the lift to the top of the Hallgrímskirkja's tower for superlative views of the city and coastline, then check out the huge church organ.

Apótek

Sundhöllin p.125. From the church, walk down to Sundhöllin swimming pool, where you can swim, bathe in the hot pots, or even sunbathe on the sun terraces if the weather allows.

Dinner p.57. Undoubtedly one of Reykjavík's most creative restaurants, *Friðrik V* features a delicious fusion of Mediterranean and Icelandic flavours.

Hallgrímskirkja

Day two in Reykjavík

Landnámssýning p.32. Inspect the remains of a Viking-age hall, still in its original location, and learn all about the days of the Settlement in this informative and engaging museum.

Saga Museum p.40. Put faces to some of the names who featured prominently during the Settlement of Iceland – the wax models in this museum are startlingly lifelike.

Lunch p.38. Sample some of the freshest fish you're ever likely to taste at the renowned *Icelandic Fish & Chips*, inside the Volcano House.

Saga Museum

Volcano House p.36. Watch the films of Icelandic eruptions in the Volcano House and witness the disruptive power Icelanders live with on a daily basis.

Laugavegur p.55. Time for some retail therapy: go for a wander along the length of Laugavegur and you might just succumb to the range of goods on offer.

Phallological Museum p.61. At the eastern end of Laugavegur, you'll find Reykjavík's most offbeat museum – dedicated to the humble penis. Examples of members from every mammal species found in Iceland (human included) abound.

Laugavegur

Dinner p.45. Classic Icelandic dishes are given a modern makeover at *Matur og Drykkur*, next to the Saga Museum.

Seafront stroll p.62. Take a post-dinner stroll along Sæbraut for some great views of Mount Esja, as well as a chance to see the iconic *Sólfar* statue and historic Höfði house.

Matur og Drykkur

Away from the crowds

Reykjavík is one of Europe's smaller and saner capitals. Escaping the crowds and finding a spot of peace and tranquillity is relatively easy.

Hafnarfjörður p.76. Hop on the bus for the short ride to Hafnarfjörður, Reykjavík's southern neighbour. In comparison with the capital, the streets here are all but empty of visitors.

Viðey p.74. For just 1100kr you can ride the ferry to Viðey for great views of Reykjavík and the surrounding coastline. Though fairly small, Viðey boasts some great hiking trails, too, offering a real chance to commune with nature in the city.

Viðey

Reykjanes Peninsula p.80. With your own transport a drive around the southwestern point of the Reykjanes Peninsula, through the lava landscapes between Grindavík and Hafnir, is especially rewarding – not least for an intercontinental bridge, steaming mud pools, and sea cliffs stacked with bird life.

Öskjuhlíð p.66. The forested slopes of this city park south of the centre are the perfect place to escape the crowds. Pack a picnic and find your own shady glade among the trees.

Reykjanes Peninsula

South of Hallgrímskirkja p.60. The streets south of Hallgrímskirkja, notably Njarðargata, Baldursgata and Óðinsgata, are relatively unexplored by visitors to the city. A stroll here is a chance to see residential Reykjavík – look for a few older houses weatherproofed in corrugated iron.

Sun terraces, Sundhöllin p.125. Sheltered from the wind, the outdoor terraces at the swimming pool here are a wonderful spot to catch the rays (in the buff) on a warm day – and they're little known to visitors.

South of Hallgrímskirkja

Eat and drink like a local

With a wide range of eating and drinking options, it can be hard to make a sound choice. Here, then, is how the locals do it.

Vínbúðin p.30 & p.74. Given the high price of alcohol in Reykjavík's bar and restaurants, many Reykjavíkers simply drink at home instead. Buy your booze from the *vínbúðin* on Austurstræti and save a small fortune.

Mokka p.65. This simple café on Skólavörðustígur is a Reykjavík classic. It's been plying the people of the city with caffeine for years – and they can't get enough of it.

Mokka

Ostabúðin p.64. Drop in to this popular little delicatessen and buy some freshly baked bread and a few nibbles for a picnic lunch – you'll feel like you've lived in Reykjavík for years.

Happy hours p.45, p.51 & p.65. Save money by drinking during the happy hours which are posted up outside many bars. A large beer can go for as little as 600kr – much less than you'd pay at home.

Vegamót p.59. The weekend brunch specials at this long-standing locals' favourite really pull the crowds. *Vegamót* is not only good value but it's also a fun place to hang out.

Sandholt p.57. Reykjavíkers claim this is the best café in the city. There's a great choice of takeaway pastries and sandwiches and its home-made chocolates are famous.

Ostabúðin

Bæjarins Beztu Pylsur p.37. Legendary mobile stand down near the seafront, which has been serving customers its trademark hot dogs smothered in fried onions and remoulade since 1937.

Kaffivagninn p.44. For great cakes and breakfasts head to this harbourside fishermen's hangout, one of Reykjavík's oldest cafés.

Sandholt

Kids' Reykjavík

Despite its small size, Reykjavík is a very child-friendly city, and whatever the weather, there's always something going on nearby to help keep children entertained.

Blue Lagoon p.80. The iconic Icelandic spa. This huge spread of milky-blue, steaming water sits among the Reykjanes Peninsula's lunar landscape of black volcanic rubble, ideal for letting off steam going to or from the airport.

Whale watching p.43. Whale-watching tours depart Reykjavík harbour throughout the year, with a fairly decent chance of seeing minke whales, white beaked dolphins and harbour porpoises – not to mention puffins and other sea birds.

Blue Lagoon

Viðey trip p.74. A brief ferry ride from Sundahöfn harbour will land you on this extinct volcano. Though little remains of the island's rich history, it's a great place to ramble along easy coastal tracks, enjoying the seascapes

Horseriding p.126. Icelandic horses are a unique breed, known for their stocky build, quiet temper and gliding *tölt* gait. Farms outside Reykjavík organize treks for all levels of experience, lasting from an hour to a day.

Saga Museum p.40. Lively waxworks illustrating key figures from the country's early history – don't miss Hrafna-Flóki, discoverer of Iceland, or the Viking-poet Egil Skallagrímsson – though be aware that some scenes are realistically brutal.

Whale watching

Tjörnin p.46. Head for the corner with Fríkirkjuvegur where graylag geese, eider ducks and even whooper swans gather, hoping for handouts. Don't miss the amazing relief map of Iceland, which fills its own room inside the nearby Ráðhúsið.

Tjörnin

Out of town

Enhance even a brief trip to Reykjavík with some raw, iconic Icelandic scenery, all within an easy hour or two's drive of the capital.

Golden Circle p.86. Classic Icelandic trio: a thundering two-tier cataract through a gorge at Gulfoss; Geysir's erupting hot springs; and the stunning Þingvellir rift valley, historic setting for Iceland's original parliament, where the country is literally tearing apart.

Heimaey p.100. This small island – home to a few thousand people and millions of seabirds – remains actively volcanic after a devastating eruption during the 1970s. Climb to the still-steaming crater rim of the Eldfell volcano for fantastic views.

Heimaey

Seljalandsfoss p.96. One of Iceland's most beautiful waterfalls, this thin ribbon cascades off a plateau's edge into a broad plunge pool. Walk around behind the curtain for unique views – and a good soaking.

Vík p.99. Iceland's only coastal town without a harbour, charming Vík sports a black volcanic sand beach, the offshore "Troll Rocks", and a looming, grassy headland thick with roosting seabird colonies.

Vík

Reynishverfi p.99. Attractive shingle beach near Iceland's southernmost point, with beautiful seascapes, basalt rock formations in nearby cliffs and resident puffins through the summer. Just be sure to take care with the dangerous surf.

Sólheimajökull p.98. One of the closest glaciers to Reykjavík, and the most accessible, where you can approach the blackened, gravel-covered snout and even try your hand at some ice-climbing (under supervision).

Sólheimajökull

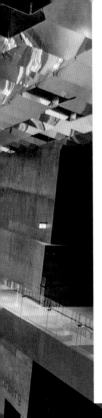

PLACES

Harpa

Lækjartorg, Austurstræti and Austurvöllur

The best place to get your first taste of Reykjavík is around Lækjartorg and the adjoining pedestrianized Austurstræti, on the square's western side. This area is a general meeting place for Reykjavík's urbanites, where people come to stroll, strut and sit on benches munching cakes, ice creams and burgers bought from the nearby fast-food outlets and the 10–11 supermarket. If Reykjavík has a main square, meanwhile, it is Austurvöllur, a more stately – though still diminutive – space south of Austurstræti that is home to the Icelandic parliament, Reykjavík cathedral and a handful of imposing buildings, including the city's very first hotel, Hótel Borg, dating from the 1930s.

Lækjartorg

MAP p.28, POCKET MAP D4

Lækjartorg square has always been at the heart of Reykjavík life; indeed, it was here that farmers bringing produce to market ended their long journey from the surrounding countryside and set up camp and sell their goods. Although the Icelandic name does indeed mean "square" ("brook square", in fact, named after the stream which flows beneath it), Lækjartorg is not the kind of grand, imposing place you might find elsewhere in Europe: it is more a wide, paved pedestrian entrance to Austurstræti.

Despite its relatively modest appearance, however, this can be one of the most boisterous areas in the city. On Friday and Saturday evenings, particularly during summertime, hundreds of drunken revellers fill the square when the clubs empty out at around 4 or 5am, jostling for prime position – the noise from the good-hearted throng can be deafening.

Austurstræti

MAP p.28, POCKET MAP D4

By day, **Austurstræti** has a busy commercial air as people dash in and out of the post office, pop in to the Eymundsson bookshop and sort out money matters at the main branch of Landsbanki. Beyond its junction with Pósthússtræti, the road gives itself over solely to pleasure, as this is where some of the city's best bars and restaurants can be found. Austurstræti is also the location for the *vínbúð* **state alcohol store**, a futuristic glass-and-steel structure at number 10a, where those who want to drink at home have to come to buy their alcohol supplies.

Austurvöllur

MAP p.28, POCKET MAP C4

Pósthússtræti, running south from Austurstræti, leads into another small square, **Austurvöllur**, a favourite place for city slickers from nearby offices to catch a few rays during their lunch breaks, stretched out on the grassy lawns edged with

Icelandic people power

Every Saturday between October 2008 and January 2009, thousands of Icelanders gathered in Austurvöllur to voice their anger over the collapse of the Icelandic banking system which, it's estimated, left one in five families bankrupt. The protesters burned the flag of Landsbanki (one of the country's leading banks) and were soon also calling for heads to roll. The main target of popular discontent was the leader of the Icelandic Central Bank and former long-serving politician, Davíð Oddsson, who was squarely blamed for the economic collapse, and was replaced as the head of the bank in March 2009. The demonstrators became more vocal as the lack of decisive action by the government continued, with three and a half months of protests in Austurvöllur and at various locations around the country finally convincing Prime Minister Geir Haarde that his administration had no future; to national jubilation, it fell on January 26, 2009. Today, thanks to the square's central position and the fact that any number of MPs regularly trot through on their way to parliamentary sessions, this remains Iceland's favourite place for demonstrators to harangue the government.

flowers. The square's modest proportions and nondescript apartment blocks, meanwhile, somewhat belie its historical importance: this was the site of the farm of Reykjavík's first settler, **Ingólfur Arnarson**; it's thought he grew his hay on the land where the square now stands, and it marks the original centre of the city. Similarly, the square's central, elevated statue of the nineteenth-century independence campaigner **Jón Sigurðsson**, entitled *The Pride of Iceland, its Sword and Shield*, faces two of the most important buildings in the country – the Alþingishúsið and the Dómkirkjan – though you'd never realize their status from their appearance.

Austurvöllur

Lækjartorg, Austurstræti and Austurvöllur

SHOPS
Eymundsson	2
Nordic Store	3
Vínbúðin	1

CAFÉS & RESTAURANTS
Apótek	4
Café Paris	3
Einar Ben	1
Grillmarkaðurinn	5
Laundromat Café	2
Nora Magasin	6

BARS
Bjarni Fel	3
English Pub	2
Micro Bar	1

ACCOMMODATION
Borg	4
Plaza	1
Radisson Blu 1919	2
Reykjavík Centrum	3

Alþingishúsið (Parliament House)

MAP ABOVE, POCKET MAP C4
Austurvöllur Square. Closed to the public.

The **Alþingishúsið** is ordinary in the extreme, a slight building made of grey basalt quarried from nearby Skólavörðuholt hill, with the date of its completion (1881) etched into its dark frontage – yet this unremarkable structure played a pivotal role in bringing about Icelandic independence. In 1798, the parliament moved to Reykjavík from Þingvellir (see p.86), where it had been operating virtually without interruption since 930 AD. Within just two years, however, it was dissolved as Danish power reached its peak. Yet after much struggle, the Alþingi regained its powers from Copenhagen as a consultative body in 1843, and a constitution was granted in 1874 which made Iceland self-governing in domestic affairs. The **Act of Union**, passed in this building in 1918, made Iceland a sovereign state under the Danish Crown, but by 1940 Denmark was occupied by the Nazis and the Alþingi had assumed the duties normally carried out by the monarch, declaring its intention to dissolve the Act of Union at the end of the war. Today, the modest interior, illuminated by chandeliers, more resembles an ordinary town council chamber than the seat of a national parliament.

Dómkirkjan

MAP ABOVE, POCKET MAP D4
Lækjargata 14a. Mon–Fri 10am–4.30pm. Free.

Reykjavík's Lutheran cathedral, the **Dómkirkjan**, is a Neoclassical stone structure partly shrouded in corrugated iron to protect it from

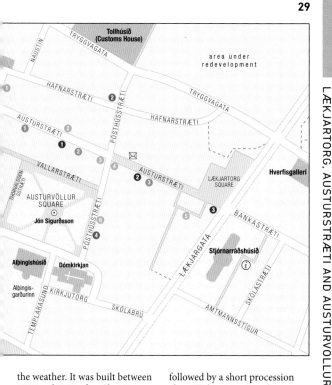

the weather. It was built between 1787 and 1796 after Christian VII of Denmark scrapped the Catholic bishoprics of Hólar in the north and Skálholt in the south, in favour of a Lutheran diocese in what was fast growing into Iceland's main centre of population. The church may be plain on the outside, but venture within and you'll discover a beautiful interior: perfectly designed arched windows punctuate the unadorned white-painted walls at regular intervals, giving an impression of complete architectural harmony. The cathedral is now deemed too small for great gatherings and services of state, and the roomier Hallgrímskirkja (see p.60) is preferred for state funerals and other such well-attended functions, although the **opening of parliament** is still marked with a service in the Dómkirkjan

followed by a short procession along Kirkjuststræti to the Alþingishúsið.

Dómkirkjan

Shops

Eymundsson

MAP p.28, POCKET MAP D4
Austurstræti 18 ☏ 540 2130,
ⓦ penninn.is. Mon–Sat 9am–10pm,
Sun 10am–10pm.

The best bookshop in Reykjavík,
Eymundsson offers a broad
selection of books about Iceland
in English as well as videos,
postcards and other souvenirs
to take home.

Nordic Store

MAP p.28, POCKET MAP D4
Lækjargata 2 ☏ 445 8080,
ⓦ nordicstore.net. Daily 9am–10pm.

A one-stop shop for anything
woollen, including extremely
cosy traditional Icelandic
jumpers. Eiderdown duvets are
also available here, and home
shipping is offered.

Vínbúðin

MAP p.28, POCKET MAP C4
Austurstræti 10a ☏ 562 6511,
ⓦ vinbudin.is. Mon–Thurs & Sat
11am–6pm, Fri 11am–7pm.

A handily located branch of
the state alcohol monopoly.
Remember that, in Iceland,
booze is sold exclusively at
vínbúðin – you'll search in
vain elsewhere.

Cafés and restaurants

Apótek

MAP p.28, POCKET MAP D4
Austurstræti 16 ☏ 551 0011,
ⓦ apotekrestaurant.is. Mon–Thurs
11.30am–11pm, Fri 11.30am–midnight,
Sat noon–midnight, Sun noon–11.30pm.

Apótek, once Reykjavík's main
apothecary, is now a stylish
restaurant specializing in fresh
seafood with a modern twist.
The set lunches (2990–3990kr)
represent a pretty good deal.

Café Paris

MAP p.28, POCKET MAP D4
Austurstræti 14 ☏ 551 1020,
ⓦ cafeparis.is. Daily: May–Aug
8am–1am; Sept–April 9am–1am.

Long gone are the days when
this was virtually the only café
in town. Since it opened in 1992,
the French-style *Café Paris* has
become a Reykjavík fixture, with
outdoor seating overlooking
the Alþingi in summer. Offers
English breakfasts for 2800kr,
as well as excellent crêpes and
refreshing salads.

Einar Ben

MAP p.28, POCKET MAP C3
Veltusund 1 ☏ 511 5090, ⓦ einarben
.is. Daily 5.30–11pm.

Named after the poet Einar
Benediktsson, this handsome
place is heavy with chandeliers
and red drape curtains. The
menu errs on the creative, side,
offering the likes of pan-fried
salmon with butternut purée
(4800kr), or cod fillet with
tomato concassé, feta cheese
and ginger (also 4800kr). An
early-bird two-course special is
available until 7pm for 4200kr.

Grillmarkaðurinn

MAP p.28, POCKET MAP D4
Lækjargata 2a ☏ 571 7777,
ⓦ grillmarkadurinn.is. Mon–Fri

Einar Ben

11.30am–2pm & 6–10.30pm, Sat & Sun 6–11.30pm.

Everything served at this stylish modern restaurant – from salmon and cod to steaks, burgers and vegetables – is sourced from local farmers and fishermen and cooked on the custom-made charcoal grill. The tasting menu, for 10,900kr per person (two people minimum), is well worth a try.

Laundromat Café

MAP p.28, POCKET MAP C3
Austurstræti 9 ☏ 587 7555, ⓦ thelaundromatcafe.com. Mon–Thurs 8am–midnight, Fri 8am–1am, Sat 9am–1am, Sun 9am–midnight.

The walls of this café are covered with maps and the bar is made of bookshelves lined with paperbacks. On the menu are burgers, salads, soups and sandwiches, plus breakfast options. Oh, and there's a laundry on site, too.

Nora Magasin

MAP p.28, POCKET MAP D4
Posthússtræti 9 ☏ 578 2010, ⓦ facebook.com/noramagasin. Mon–Thurs & Sun 11.30am–1am, Fri & Sat 11.30am–3am.

This place may be searching for an identity when it comes to decor – part family sitting room and part trendy urban bar – but the food is just plain good: burgers (2490kr), sandwiches (1850kr) and a tasty fish of the day (2490kr).

Bars

Bjarni Fel

MAP p.28, POCKET MAP D4
Austurstræti 20 ☏ 561 2240. Mon–Thurs & Sun noon–1am, Fri & Sat noon–4.30am.

With its no-music policy, this small and intimate sports bar, full of memorabilia and TV screens angled in all directions,

Nora Magasin

is the best place to catch the latest football match over a cold beer or two.

English Pub

MAP p.28, POCKET MAP D4
Austurstræti 12 ☏ 578 0400, ⓦ enskibarinn.is. Mon–Thurs & Sun noon–1am, Fri & Sat noon–4.30am.

This is an attempt to create a British-style pub in the heart of Reykjavík, and while the interior is none too genuine, there's lager, Guinness and Kilkenny on draught, lots of footie on TV and live music at the weekend. You can also try spinning the "wheel of fortune", with up to eight free beers as the prize if you win.

Micro Bar

MAP p.28, POCKET MAP C3
Austurstræti 6 ☏ 571 1400, ⓦ citycenterhotel.is. Daily noon–midnight.

Attached to the *City Center* hotel, this place is a real treat. Micro Bar serves eighty or so different beers from around the world, plus a good selection produced by some of Iceland's microbreweries. From pale ales to barley wines, and from stouts to lagers, you're bound to find a tipple to please.

Aðalstræti, Hafnarstræti and Tryggvagata

The trio of streets, Aðalstræti, Hafnarstræti and Tryggvagata, contains many of Reykjavík's bars and tourist-oriented shops. Don't confuse them, though, with the grand boulevards you might find in other capital cities; instead, they're modest affairs, barely a couple of hundred metres in length. Although they can't compete with Laugavegur, the city's main shopping street (see p.55), which is an altogether busier thoroughfare, these three are arguably a more pleasant place to stroll and linger. You'll doubtless end up spending time here either heading for the tourist office in Aðalstræti, sampling the shopping and bar culture or passing through on your way to the harbour. It's also where you'll find a couple of the city's museums, which come as a welcome addition to the shops and restaurants.

Aðalstræti

MAP p.34, POCKET MAP C4

From the southwestern corner of Austurvöllur, Kirkjustræti runs the short distance to Reykjavík's oldest street, **Aðalstræti**, which follows the route taken in the late ninth century by Ingólfur Arnarson (see p.131) from his farm at the southern end of the street down to the sea. In addition to the remains of a Viking-age farmhouse on display inside the Landnámssýning museum, Aðalstræti also holds Reykjavík's **oldest surviving building**, a squat timber structure at no. 10. It dates back to 1752, and has served as a weaving shed, a bishop's residence and the home of Skúli Magnússon, High Sheriff of Iceland, who encouraged the development of craft industries here. On the opposite side of the street, a few steps north towards the sea outside the present no. 9, is Ingólfur Arnarson's freshwater well, **Ingólfsbrunnur**, which was discovered by fluke during road repairs here in 1992 and is now glassed over for posterity.

Landnámssýning (Settlement Exhibition)

MAP p.34, POCKET MAP C4

Aðalstræti 16 ☎ 411 6372, ⊛ borgarso .gusafn.is/en. Daily 9am–6pm. 1600kr.

The **Landnámssýning**, whose centrepiece is the extensive ruins of a **Viking-age farmhouse**, is one of Reykjavík's most remarkable museums. Housed in a purpose-built hall directly beneath Aðalstræti, the structure's oval-shaped stone walls, excavated in 2001, enclose a sizeable living space of 85 square metres, with a central hearth as the focal point. Dating the farmhouse has been quite straightforward, since the layer of volcanic ash which fell across Iceland following a powerful eruption in around 871 AD lies just beneath the building;

Aðalstræti 10

it's estimated, therefore, that people lived here between 930 and 1000 AD. The exhibition's wall space is given over to panoramic views of forest and scrubland to convey a realistic impression of what Reykjavík would have looked like at the time of the Settlement. Indeed, when the first settlers arrived in the area, the hills were covered in birch woods. However, just one hundred years later, the birch had all but disappeared, felled to make way for grazing land or burnt for charcoal needed for iron-smelting.

Housed in a side room to the left of reception, the **Saga Exhibition** is the place to see some of Iceland's medieval documents. Sadly, there are only five manuscripts on display here (the *Book of Icelanders*, the *Saga of the People of Kjalarnes*, the *Book of Settlements*, *Jónsbók* and the Deed of Purchase for Reykjavík from 1615) and you're bound to leave with your appetite barely whetted. However, if construction of Hús íslenskra fræða (House of Icelandic Studies), opposite the

National Museum (see p.48), is completed several years hence, this modest display will close and a more comprehensive exhibition will open in its place in the new building, which will also house the Árni Magnússon Institute, the keeper of Iceland's medieval manuscripts.

Landnámssýning

SHOPS
Kolaportið	1
Puffin	3
The Viking	2

CAFÉS & RESTAURANTS
Bæjarins Beztu Pylsur	5
Fish Market	7
Grillhúsið	3
Hornið	6
Icelandic Fish & Chips	2
Restaurant Reykjavik	4
Reykjavik Fish Restaurant	1

BARS
Dubliner	3
Frederiksen Ale House	2
Gaukurinn	1
Tivoli	4

N

**Aðalstræti,
Hafnarstræti
and Tryggvagata**

Hafnarstræti

MAP ABOVE, POCKET MAP D3

Many of the buildings on the south
side of **Hafnarstræti** were formerly
owned by Danish merchants during
the 1602–1855 Trade Monopoly.
Indeed, this street, as its name
suggests (*hafnar* means "harbour"),
once bordered the sea and gave
access to the harbour, the city's
economic lifeline and means of
contact with the outside world.
Today, Hafnarstræti is several
blocks from the ocean, after landfill
extended the city foreshore, and
is home to some excellent bars
and restaurants. Together with
Austurstræti to the south and
Tryggvagata to the north, it forms
part of a rectangular block of cafés,
restaurants and drinking holes that
are well worth exploring.

Fálkahúsið

MAP ABOVE, POCKET MAP C3

Corner of Aðalstræti and Hafnarstræti.

Opposite the tourist office, and
covered in corrugated iron for
protection, **Fálkahúsið** is another
of Reykjavík's beautifully restored
timber buildings, one of three in
the city where the King of Denmark
once kept his much-prized
Icelandic falcons. Its turret-like side
walls and sheer size still impress,
especially when you consider the
huge amount of timber that was
imported for the job, as Iceland had
no trees of its own. Cast an eye to
the roof and you'll spot two carved
wooden falcons still keeping guard
over the building.

Tryggvagata

MAP ABOVE, POCKET MAP D3

Tryggvagata, one block north
of the bustle of Hafnarstræti, is
remarkable for a few things other
than the number of consonants
in its name. The imposing,
multicoloured mosaic **mural** by
Gerður Helgadóttir (1928–75) close

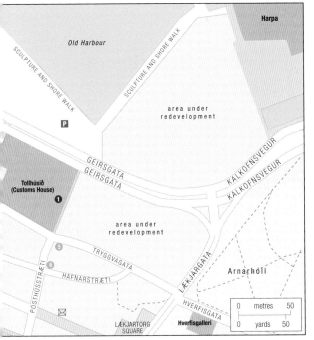

to its junction with Pósthússtræti portrays a busy harbour scene complete with fishing trawlers and cranes, and livens up the otherwise dull Tollhúsið (Customs House). Also along here are Ljósmindasafn – Reykjavík's Museum of Photography – and Hafnarhúsið, part of the Reykjavík Art Museum.

Ljósmindasafn (Photography Museum)

MAP ABOVE, POCKET MAP C3
Tryggvagata 15 ☏ 411 6300,
🌐 borgarsogusafn.is/en. Mon–Thurs
10am–6pm, Fri 11am–6pm, Sat & Sun
1–5pm. 1000kr.

The top floor of the city library building, **Grófarhús**, is given over to a changing exhibition of contemporary photography. Though the space is modest, **Ljósmindasafn** holds an impressive collection of around six million photographs which it showcases alongside work from established visiting photographers. Moreover, the entire collection, which spans from 1870 to 2002, can now also be viewed online through the museum's website.

Ljósmindasafn

Hafnarhúsið

Hafnarhúsið (Harbour House)

MAP p.34, POCKET MAP C3
Tryggvagata 17 411 6400,
artmuseum.is. Daily 10am–5pm,
Thurs till 10pm. 1400kr.

The large, austere **Hafnarhúsið** was originally constructed in the 1930s as warehouse storage and office space for the Port of Reykjavík, but has now been converted into six large exhibition halls, connected by a corridor running over a central courtyard. The museum plays host to frequently changing displays of contemporary Icelandic and international art, with one permanent exhibition dedicated to the multicoloured, cartoon-like work of Icelandic pop artist Erró. There's certainly plenty of space here, but the overall layout is a little confusing, with an array of corridors – which once linked the former warehouse's storage areas – that twist and turn around the museum's supporting concrete and steel pillars.

Volcano House

MAP p.34, POCKET MAP C2
Tryggvagata 11 volcanohouse.is.
Daily 10am–10pm. 1990kr.

Unless you're of a serious geological bent, it's unlikely you'll to want to give but the merest of glances to the lumps of pumice, tephra and jasper displayed here. Actually more cinema than museum, the **Volcano House** is worth visiting mostly for the twenty-minute films of the 1973 Westman Islands and 2010 Eyjafjallajökull eruptions, shown every hour on the hour. Although rather grainy, the Westman Islands film is the more interesting of the two, documenting the devastating impact of the eruption on the island community. The Eyjafjallajökull film, while outlining the basics of what happened geologically during the eruption, barely mentions the ensuing chaos in the skies across Europe.

Art for sale

With so much art on display in this relatively small city, it can be tempting to purchase an original Icelandic work while you're in Reykjavík. Should the urge strike, there are two galleries worth checking out where you'll find a range of artists and styles represented: the long-established **i8**, at Tryggvagata 18 (551 3666, i8.is; Tues–Fri 11am–6pm, Sat 1–5pm; free) works with a group of around twenty artists, both Icelandic and international, who produce contemporary fine art; at **Hverfisgallerí**, just a few blocks away at Hverfisgata 4 (537 4007, hverfisgalleri.is; Tues–Fri 1–5pm, Sat & Sun 2–5pm; free), all bar one of the seventeen artists represented are Icelandic, and the style is again contemporary fine art. Exhibitions at both galleries tend to run for around five weeks.

Kolaportið

Shops

Kolaportið

MAP p.34, POCKET MAP D3
Tryggvagata 19 🕿 562 5030, ⓦ kolaportid
.is. Sat & Sun 11am–5pm.
Iceland's biggest flea market is
housed in a cavernous building
where you'll find any number of
secondhand and new items. There's
also a food section that, among
other things, stocks unusual
delicacies such as shark meat.

Puffin

MAP p.34, POCKET MAP C3
Hafnarstræti 5 🕿 519 6070. Daily
10am–5pm.
Fun, tourist-oriented clothes
store selling all manner of
T-shirts, caps, hats, woollen
sweaters and the like, as well
as Iceland souvenirs.

The Viking

MAP p.34, POCKET MAP C3
Hafnarstræti 1–3 🕿 551 1250, ⓦ theviking
.is. Mon, Thurs & Fri 9am–9pm, Tues &
Wed 9am–8pm, Sat 9am–10pm, Sun
10am–8pm.
From pens to fridge magnets,
sheepskin rugs to woollen
sweaters, this popular souvenir
shop's got it covered. There's also a
collection of books about Iceland,
plus postcards.

Cafés and restaurants

Bæjarins Beztu Pylsur

MAP p.34, POCKET MAP D3
Tryggvagata 1 🕿 511 1566, ⓦ bbp.is.
Daily 10am–1am, Fri & Sat till 4.30am.
Hidden away on a patch of waste
ground between Tryggvagata
and Hafnarstræti, *Bæjarins* is a
local institution, having opened
in 1937. From a small kiosk they
serve up the Nordic classic: a *pýlsa*
(hot dog; 400kr), with lashings of
fried onion and thick remoulade
sauce. Be prepared to queue.

The Viking

Fish Market

MAP p.34, POCKET MAP C4
Aðalstræti 12 ☎ 578 8877,
Ⓦ fiskmarkadurinn.is. Mon–Fri
11.30am–2pm & 6–11.30pm, Sat &
Sun 6–11.30pm.

Smart, stylish restaurant heavy
on fake greenery and specializing
in dishes given an Asian twist –
try grilled blue ling (5700kr) or
the angelica-fed organic lamb
(6800kr). All produce is bought
direct from Icelandic fishermen
and farmers.

Grillhúsið

MAP p.34, POCKET MAP C3
Tryggvagata 20 ☎ 527 5000, Ⓦ grillhusid
.is. Mon–Thurs 11.30am–10pm, Fri & Sat
11.30am–11pm.

Popular and informal grill
restaurant, particularly busy at
weekends, decked out to resemble
an American diner. The menu
runs to pricey steaks, but it's best
for its burgers (from 1990kr) and
fish and chips (2590kr).

Hornið

MAP p.34, POCKET MAP D3
Hafnarstræti 15 ☎ 551 3340, Ⓦ hornid.is.
Daily 11am–11.30pm.

Another classic Reykjavík
restaurant that's stood the test
of time – this one has been here

Hornið

Fish Market

since 1979 and is popular for the
excellent pizzas (around 2490kr)
and pasta (around 2990kr). They
also do a good range of meat and
fish dishes, such as salmon with
garlic (4290kr) and a succulent
lamb fillet (5190kr).

Icelandic Fish & Chips

MAP p.34, POCKET MAP C2
Tryggvagata 11 ☎ 511 1118,
Ⓦ fishandchips.is. Daily 11.30am–9.30pm.

Proper sit-down restaurant in the
Volcano House (see p.36) serving
exactly what you'd expect from the
name. The type of fish available
varies daily (1390–1590kr), but
the sides don't – whatever you
choose, simply add fries, onion
rings or salad, or other garnishes
such as delicious home-made dips.

Restaurant Reykjavík

MAP p.34, POCKET MAP C3
Vesturgata 2 ☎ 552 3030,
Ⓦ restaurantreykjavik.is. Daily
11.30am–9.30pm.

This minimalist-smart restaurant
has long been a popular standby
for its accomplished lamb and fish
dishes, but their real showpiece
is the evening seafood buffet
(from 5.30pm; 6950kr), featuring
everything from smoked salmon
through to traditional Icelandic
fish stew. Bookings essential.

Reykjavík Fish Restaurant

MAP p.34, POCKET MAP B2
Tryggvagata 8 ☎ 578 5656,
ⓦ reykjavikfish.is. Daily 11am–10pm.
Another of Reykjavík's restaurants
catering to the current craze for
British-style fish and chips – here
you can choose tangy sauces to go
with them, such as mango chilli or
lemon pepper and dill. There's also
a great smoked salmon salad, fish
soup, and delicious Arctic char
with potato salad.

Bars

Dubliner

MAP p.34, POCKET MAP C3
Naustin 1 ☎ 527 3232. Mon & Tues 4pm–
midnight, Wed 4pm–1am, Thurs 3pm–1am,
Fri 3pm–4.30am, Sat 1pm–4.30am, Sun
1pm–midnight.
Iceland's first-ever Irish pub still
draws in the crowds. It's always a
good choice for an evening pint,
and there's a reasonable selection
of whiskeys, plus live music (often
Irish folk and R&B) every night.

Frederiksen Ale House

MAP p.34, POCKET MAP C3
Hafnarstræti 5 ☎ 571 0055, ⓦ frederiksen
.is. Mon–Thurs & Sun noon–1am, Fri & Sat
noon–5am.

Restaurant Reykjavík

This well-located pub is busy at
any time of day. There's a decent
selection of draught and bottled
beers, including Víking classic,
Thule and stout. The expert staff
are also adept at knocking up
wicked cocktails.

Gaukurinn

MAP p.34, POCKET MAP C3
Tryggvagata 22 ☎ 781 7273, ⓦ gaukurinn
.is. Wed & Thurs 9pm–1am, Fri & Sat
9pm–4.30am.
Long-established, though recently
renovated, this live music venue
and bar has been drawing the
crowds since even before beer was
legalized in 1989. You'll find a mix
of live music, karaoke, open mic
nights and pub quiz events (see
the website for details).

Tivoli

MAP p.34, POCKET MAP C3
Hafnarstræti 4 ☎ 555 2600. Wed & Thurs
8pm–1am, Fri & Sat 8pm–4.30am.
This cool and intimate little lounge
bar, with bare brick walls, stripped
pine floors and rather plush
booths, is especially well known
for its cocktails. Throw in some
accomplished DJs and you've got
a popular place with the suave
young crowd who come here to
dance and be seen.

ADALSTRÆTI, HAFNARSTRÆTI AND TRYGGVAGATA

The harbour

North of Geirsgata, the busy main road which runs parallel to the shoreline, lies Reykjavík harbour, built around reclaimed land – the beach where vessels once unloaded their foreign goods is now well inland from here. Street names in this area, such as Ægisgata (Ocean Street) and Öldugata (Wave Street), reflect the importance of the sea to the city, and a stroll along the dockside demonstrates Iceland's dependence on the Atlantic, with fishing trawlers being checked over and prepared for their next battle against the waves, and plastic crates of ice-packed cod awaiting transportation to village stores around the country. Keep an eye out, too, for the black whaling ships, each with a red "H" painted on its funnel (hvalur is Icelandic for "whale"), which are usually moored here. Ironically, the harbour is also the departure point for whale-watching and puffin-spotting tours.

Saga Museum

MAP OPPOSITE, POCKET MAP A1
Grandagarður 2 ☎ 511 1517,
🔲 sagamuseum.is. Daily 10am–6pm.
2100kr.

Housed in a former fish storehouse on the western edge of the harbour, the excellent **Saga Museum** is Iceland's answer to Madame Tussauds. The expertly crafted wax models of characters from the sagas and their reconstructed farms and homes are employed, superbly, to depict medieval Icelandic life, often a misunderstood period in the country's history.

A visit here will give you a sense

Saga Museum

of what life must have been like in Iceland centuries ago, and all the big names are here: poet and historian **Snorri Sturluson** (see p.94), who even breathes deeply as he ponders; Eirík the Red; and explorer Leifur Eiríksson (see p.60) and his sister Freydís, the latter portrayed slicing off her breast as a solitary stand against the natives of Vínland who, after killing one of her compatriots, turned on her – according to the sagas, Freydís's actions saw her aggressors immediately take flight.

An informative audioguide (included in the admission fee) explains a little about each of the characters on display – and also about the smells of the period, which have been synthetically reproduced inside, too.

Sjóminjasafn (Maritime Museum)

MAP ABOVE, POCKET MAP M1
Grandagardur 8 ☎ 411 6300, ⊕ maritime museum.is. Daily 10am–5pm. Museum 1600kr; Ódinn 1300kr; 2400kr for both.

Given Iceland's prominence as a seafaring nation, Reykjavík's **Maritime Museum** is a big disappointment. A ragtag collection of old fishing hooks, dried fish and model boats, this tired exhibition of fisheries through the ages is dull in the extreme. The only saving grace is the former coastguard vessel, *Ódinn*, moored in the dock outside (daily guided tours at 1pm, 2pm & 3pm). Built in Denmark in 1959, the ship patrolled Iceland's territorial waters in the North Atlantic until 2006, taking part in all three cod wars with the UK. The cutters used to slice through the nets of British trawlers are displayed on *Ódinn*'s rear deck. Note that you can peep at *Ódinn* without actually entering the museum: it's visible from the rear of the site.

Whales of Iceland

Whales of Iceland

MAP p.41, POCKET MAP M1
Fiskislóð 23 ⓦ whalesoficeland.is. Daily:
10am–5pm; Oct–April 9am–6pm. 2900kr.
This creative museum has drawn
plenty of criticism over its entry
price, but it offers a unique
opportunity (in Iceland) to
appreciate the full magnificence
of these massive marine
mammals, whose true bulk is
hidden beneath the surface of the
water. Located in a vast purpose-
built warehouse, the museum
contains 23 life-size models
suspended from the ceiling;
walking among them gives an
amazing perspective on their
sheer size. Exceptionally well
executed, with steel skeletons
and silicon skins, the models
were made in China and shipped
to Iceland in sections – the blue
whale, for example, is as long as
a tennis court. Virtually every
species found in Icelandic waters
is represented: the sperm whale,
humpback, minke and even
beluga are all here.

Harpa

MAP p.41, POCKET MAP E2
Austurbakki 2 ⓦ harpa.is. Daily 8am–
midnight. Free.
A striking addition to the
Reykjavík skyline, the eye-
catching **Harpa** opera house
had a difficult birth. At the time
of the economic crash in 2008,
the structure was barely half
built and a host of politicians
and decision-makers called
for the scheme to be scrapped,
arguing that Iceland shouldn't
be building something so
opulent in the circumstances.
Amid much derision, however,
the project went ahead and has
produced one of the city's most
memorable buildings. Taking
its cue from Iceland's unusual

Harpa

geological forms, Harpa's exterior is composed of hexagonal glass cubes, designed to resemble the basalt columns of lava seen all over the country; during the dark winter months, light shows illuminate the glass panels, producing ingenious displays of colour and shapes. The main feature of the airy interior is the classic, shoebox-shaped concert hall, **Eldborg**, with seating for up to 1800. The country's premier venue for concerts and theatre productions, Harpa is also home to the Icelandic symphony orchestra and national opera. Visitors are free to wander around the building at leisure, and the café on the ground floor makes an agreeable place to watch the comings and goings of the harbour through the hexagonal windows.

Whale watching, puffin spotting and sea angling

Whale watching

Tours leave throughout the year (up to twelve departures daily depending on the season), sailing for Faxaflói bay north of Reykjavík. You're most likely to encounter minke whales, white-beaked dolphins and harbour porpoises, though orcas, humpbacks and dolphins can also be spotted; blue, fin and sei whales will also occasionally put in an appearance. You can check the success rate of sightings on previous trips on the company websites below, and should you fail to see any whales or dolphins on your tour, the companies will offer you a free trip, which can be taken at any time within the next two years.

Puffin spotting

Between mid-May and mid-August (after which the birds head out to sea for the winter months), there are twice-daily tours around the islands of Lundey and Akurey, where puffins gather to breed in the summer. Although it's not possible to go ashore, you'll have a great view of the cliffs and grassy slopes which make up the islands' sides, and the burrows where the puffins live. Remember, though, that puffin numbers have fallen in recent years due to a lack of the birds' main source of food, the sand eel. It's a good idea to ask about the tide conditions before choosing a departure because the boats get closer to the islands on a high tide.

Sea angling

Between May and August, sea-angling tours depart three times daily from the harbour, giving you a chance to try out your deep-sea skills – you get to keep anything you catch. Catfish, cod, haddock, mackerel and pollack are the most commonly landed, and you can barbecue your catch on board, should you choose. Alternatively, you can take it to the *MAR* restaurant (see p.44), where they will cook it for you (included in the trip cost).

Operators

Recommended operators include Elding on Ægisgarður (☎519 5000, ⓦelding.is), who offer whale watching (10,990kr), puffin spotting (6500kr) and sea angling (14,200kr); and Special Tours, also on Ægisgarður (☎560 8800, ⓦspecialtours.is), who offer the same activities: whale watching (10,990kr); puffin spotting (5700kr); and sea angling (13,000kr).

Shop

Epal

MAP p.41, POCKET MAP E2
Inside Harpa concert hall, Austurbakki 2
☎ 515 7733, ⓦ epal.is. Mon–Fri
10am–6pm, Sat 11am–4pm.

A good stop if you're in
the market for items from
Scandinavia's top design houses
such as Normann Copenhagen,
Design House Stockholm,
Marimekko and Iittala.

Cafés and restaurants

Búllan

MAP p.41, POCKET MAP B2
Geirsgata 1 ☎ 511 1888, ⓦ bullan.is.
Daily 11.30am–9pm.

This unimpressive little 1950s
concrete bunker of a building at
the harbour feels like an American
diner inside – and they serve
almost nothing but burgers
(around 1200kr) and excellent
fries. Expect to queue.

Café Haiti

MAP p.41, POCKET MAP C2
Geirsgata 7c ☎ 588 8484, ⓦ cafehaiti.is.
Mon–Thurs 6am–9pm, Fri 6am–10pm, Sat
7am–10pm, Sun 7am–8pm.

Run by the effervescent Elda, who
grew up and lived in Haiti until
meeting her late Icelandic husband,
this funky café offers home-roasted
coffee as well as some delicious
soups. Holds frequent art exhibits
and live music events, too.

Fish & Chips Vagninn

MAP p.41, POCKET MAP B1
On the seafront at the junction of
Rastargata and Hlésgata ☎ 840 4100,
ⓦ fishandchipsvagninn.is. Daily
11am–9pm.

Owned by three Icelandic
families who have all lived and
worked in the UK in the seafood

Matur og Drykkur

business, this mobile trailer serves
deliciously fresh, British-style
takeaway fish and chips (1590kr)
– the fish is Icelandic, the chips
are from Dutch potatoes and
the trailer is from Leeds in West
Yorkshire. There are a few alfresco
tables and chairs, too.

Kaffivagninn

MAP p.41, POCKET MAP M1
Grandagarður 10 ☎ 551 5932,
ⓦ kaffivagninn.is. Daily 7.30am–10pm,
Sat & Sun from 9am.

Claiming to be the oldest eating
establishment in Reykjavík, this
fishermen's café down in the
harbour is great for breakfast
(served till 11am) or weekend
brunch (11.30am–3pm). They
also specialize in Danish-style
open sandwiches as well as
serving a wide range of cakes.

MAR

MAP p.41, POCKET MAP C2
Geirsgata 9 ☎ 519 5050, ⓦ marrestaurant
.com. Daily 11.30am–11pm.

Named after the Latin word for
"sea", MAR is a top-notch fish
restaurant offering a creative
menu which combines fresh
Icelandic seafood with the
flavours of the Mediterranean and
Caribbean: marinated scallops in
a coconut and lime sauce; pan-
fried cod with mustard, sesame
seeds and a tomato and lime salsa;

mussel soup with pickled carrot. Mains around 3300kr.

Matur og Drykkur

MAP p.41, POCKET MAP A1
Grandagarður 2 ☏ 571 8877,
ⓦ maturogdrykkur.is. Daily 6–11pm,
also Mon–Sat 11.30am–5pm.

Inside the Saga Museum building, this inventive restaurant, plainly decked out with a concrete floor and wooden tables, has a truly unusual menu, featuring items such as an entire baked cod's head, with throat muscles in batter on the side. Lunch a la carte (mains around 2200kr), dinner set menu (7990kr).

Sægreifinn

MAP p.41, POCKET MAP B2
Geirsgata 8 ☏ 553 1500, ⓦ saegreifinn.is.
Daily 11.30am–11pm.

This harbourside fishmonger-cum-restaurant might look unimpressive from the outside –just a pale green weatherboard shack – but it's a favourite haunt of locals who know the lobster soup (1650kr) is the best in town. There's plenty of seasonal fresh fish on the menu, too, such as halibut, which is served on skewers.

Sjávarbarinn

MAP p.41, POCKET MAP M1
Grandagarður 9 ☏ 517 3131,
ⓦ sjavarbarinn.is. Mon–Fri 9am–9pm,
Sat 10am–10pm, Sun 4–10pm.

Handy for the Saga and Maritime museums, this little fish place really comes into its own at lunchtime, when there's a seafood buffet for just 3900kr, featuring a range of fish dishes, a bowl of soup, and coffee.

Bars

Forrétta Barinn

MAP p.41, POCKET MAP B2
Nýlendugata 14 ☏ 517 1800,
ⓦ forrettabarinn.is. Daily 4pm–11pm

With a lengthy happy hour (daily 4–8pm), this funky bar serves a good range of beers from Icelandic brewery Kaldi, as well as international brands like Stella, Hoegaarden, Pilsner Urquell and Leffe. During happy hour, you can get a beer here from 500kr.

SKÝ Lounge & Bar

MAP p.41, POCKET MAP F3
Inside Centerhotel Arnarhvoll, Ingólfsstræti 1 ☏ 595 8545, ⓦ skylounge.is. Daily 11.30am–midnight.

Sip a cocktail at this rooftop bar – part of the *Centerhotel* – while enjoying superb views out towards the opera house and all the way to Mount Esja. They run a daily happy hour (5–7pm) and rustle up well-prepared canapés and a few more substantial bar snacks, such as BLT and club sandwiches.

Slippbarinn

MAP p.41, POCKET MAP B1
Mýrargata 2–8 ☏ 560 8080, ⓦ slippbarinn .is. Mon–Thurs & Sun 11.30am–midnight, Fri & Sat 11.30am–1am.

This swanky and sophisticated place, inside the *Icelandair Reykjavík Marina* hotel (see p.113), has to be the most novel location for a bar in the whole of town – right beside the slipway where the ships come in to be repainted and repaired.

Sægreifinn

Tjörnin and around

From the harbour, Pósthússtræti leads south past the bars and restaurants of Tryggvagata, Hafnarstræti and Austurstræti to Tjörnin, which is invariably translated into English as "the lake" or "the pond". Tjörn and its genitive form of tjarnar are actually old Viking words, still used in northern English dialects as "tarn" to denote a mountain lake. Originally a lagoon inside the reef that once occupied the spot where Hafnarstræti now runs, this sizeable body of water, roughly a couple of square kilometres in size, is populated by forty to fifty varieties of birds – including the notorious arctic tern, known for their dive-bombing attacks on passers-by, which are found at the lake's quieter southern end. The precise numbers of the lake's bird population are charted on noticeboards stationed at several points along the bank.

Ráðhúsið (City Hall)

MAP OPPOSITE, POCKET MAP C5
Tjarnargata 11. Mon–Fri 8am–8pm,
Sat & Sun noon–6pm. Free.

Occupying prime position on the northern edge of Tjörnin is **Ráðhúsið**. Opened in 1992, it's a showpiece of Nordic design, a modernist rectangular structure of steel, glass and chrome that actually sits on the lake itself. Inside, in addition to the city's administration offices, is a small café and, in one of the small exhibition areas, a fabulous self-standing **topographical model** of Iceland that gives an excellent impression of the country's

Ráðhúsið

Tjörnin and around

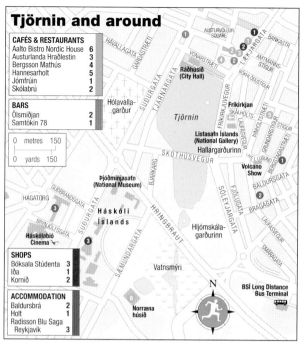

CAFÉS & RESTAURANTS

Aalto Bistro Nordic House	6
Austurlanda Hraðlestin	3
Bergsson Mathús	4
Hannesarholt	5
Jómfrúin	1
Skólabrú	2

BARS

Ölsmiðjan	2
Samtökin 78	1

SHOPS

Bóksala Stúdenta	3
Iða	1
Kornið	2

ACCOMMODATION

Baldursbrá	1
Holt	2
Radisson Blu Saga Reykjavík	3

unforgiving geography – you can marvel at the sheer size of the Vatnajökull glacier in the southeast (as big as the English county of Yorkshire) and the table mountains of the West Fjords, and gain instant respect for the people who live amid such challenging landscapes.

Suðurgata

MAP ABOVE, POCKET MAP B5

One of the best views of Reykjavík can be had from **Suðurgata**, a street running parallel to Tjörnin's western shore; to get there from the City Hall, walk west along Vonarstræti, crossing Tjarnargata. Suðurgata is lined with tidy little dwellings, but from it you can see across the lake to the city centre's suburban houses, whose corrugated-iron roofs, ranging in colour from a pallid two-tone green to bright blues and reds, have been carefully maintained by their owners – the familiar picture-postcard view of Reykjavík.

Statue overlooking Tjörnin

Þjóðminjasafn (National Museum)

MAP p.47, POCKET MAP A7
Suðurgata 41 ☏ 530 2200,
ⓦ thjodminjasafn.is. Daily 10am–5pm.
2000kr.

By far the most engaging part of the **Þjóðminjasafn** is the **first floor**, which covers the period from 800 to 1600; the video presentation within the "Origin of Icelanders" exhibition, devoted to the early Viking period and the use of DNA testing, is particularly good. Recent genetic research has shown that whereas around eighty percent of today's Icelanders are of Nordic origin, sixty-two percent of the early Viking-era women originated from the British Isles; the conclusion reached is that the first settlers sailed from Scandinavia to Iceland, stopping off at the British Isles along the way to marry.

Another prime exhibit is the small human figure, about the size of a thumb and made of bronze, which is thought to be over a thousand years old and to portray either the Norse god Þór or Christ. More spectacular is the carved church door from Valþjófsstaður in Fljótsdalur, dating from around 1200, and depicting the medieval tale *Le Chevalier au Lion*: it features an ancient warrior on horseback slugging it out with an unruly dragon. The Danish authorities finally gave up the treasure in 1930 and returned the door to Iceland, together with a host of medieval manuscripts. Check out, too, the impressive Romanesque-style carved Madonna dating from around 1200, which hails from northern Iceland and is displayed within the "Medieval church" section.

The **second floor** of the museum, devoted to the period from 1600 onwards, canters through key events in Icelandic history such as the Trade Monopoly (1602–1787) and the birth of the republic. The displays conclude with a revolving airport-style conveyor belt laden with twentieth-century appliances and knick-knacks, featuring everything from a Björk LP to a milking machine.

Þjóðminjasafn

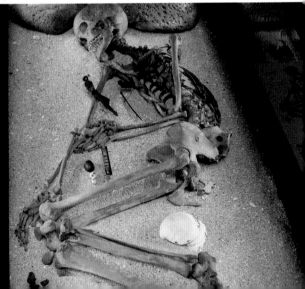

Listasafn Íslands (National Gallery)

MAP p.47, POCKET MAP D6
Fríkirkjuvegur 7 ⓣ 515 9600, ⓦ listasafn.is. Mid-Sept to mid-May Tues–Sun 11am–5pm; rest of year daily 10am–5pm. 1500kr.

A few minutes' walk north from the National Museum down Sóleyjargata, which runs along the eastern side of Tjörnin, passing the offices of the Icelandic president at the corner of Skothúsvegur, is the **Fríkirkjan** (Free Lutheran Church). The best feature of this simple wooden structure, painted whitish grey, is its high green roof and tall tower, useful as a landmark to guide you to the neighbouring former ice house, known as **Herðubreið**. Once a storage place for massive chunks of ice, hewn in winter from the frozen lake and used to preserve fish stocks, the building has been enlarged and completely redesigned, and houses **Listasafn Íslands** (the National Gallery of Iceland). Icelandic art may lack worldwide recognition, but all the significant names are to be found here, including Erró, Jón Stefánsson, Ásgrímur Jónsson, Guðmundur Þorsteinsson and Einar Hákonarson – though, disappointingly, lack of space (there are only three small exhibition rooms containing barely twenty or so paintings each) means that the works can only be shown in strictly rationed portions from the museum's enormous stock of around eleven thousand pieces of art. You can get an idea of the paintings not on display by glancing through the postcards sold at reception.

Listasafn Íslands

All aboard!

Next stop, Reykjavík Central Station... As curious as it sounds in a country prone to any number of earth tremors and eruptions, plans to build a **railway line** from central Reykjavík to Keflavík airport by 2024 are being seriously considered. Due to its inhospitable terrain and low population, Iceland is one of the few European countries not to have a rail network of any kind. However, if plans get the go-ahead, that will all change, with a high-speed track laid across the lavafields of the Reykjanes Peninsula, drastically reducing the journey time to the international airport and cutting exhaust emissions. Although no site has been officially earmarked for a train station in Reykjavík, the favourite remains the rather ramshackle BSÍ bus terminal, which could then be transformed into a modern transport interchange fit for a capital city. Currently, the bus station is owned by Reykjavík Excursions who operate the Flybus to Keflavík airport.

Shops

Bóksala Stúdenta

MAP p.47, POCKET MAP M3
Sæmundurgata 4 ☏ 570 0777,
🌐 boksala.is. Mon–Fri 9am–5pm.

This bookshop, which belongs to the university, is probably the best-stocked in the whole of Iceland. It holds a wide range of teach-yourself-Icelandic texts, as well as glossy coffee-table books about the country.

Iða

MAP p.47, POCKET MAP D4
Lækjargata 2a ☏ 511 5001, 🌐 ida.is.
Daily 9am–10pm.

Engaging gift store selling a range of tasteful souvenirs from Iceland. Also doubles as a mini-bookshop with a selection of travel guides and other books about the country.

Kornið

MAP p.47, POCKET MAP D4
Lækjargata 4 ☏ 564 1800, 🌐 kornid.is.
Mon–Fri 7am–5.30pm, Sat & Sun 7am–5pm.

This popular bakery-cum-café, a mere stone's throw from Tjörnin, specializes in fresh breads, other baked goods and good coffee, and offers outdoor seating in summer along the pavement of Lækjargata.

Cafés and restaurants

Aalto Bistro Nordic House

MAP p.47, POCKET MAP M3
Sturlugata 5 ☏ 551 0200, 🌐 nordice.is.
Mon, Tues & Sun 11am–5pm, Wed–Sat 11.30am–9.30pm.

Located in the Nordic House, a Nordic cultural centre, this new bistro operates under TV chef Sveinn Kjartansson, who mixes Icelandic and central European cuisines: how about hot-smoked catfish on a citrus salad with wild angelica mayonnaise, or some lavender and orange cake topped with *skyr* (Icelandic yoghurt)?

Austurlanda Hraðlestin

MAP p.47, POCKET MAP D4
Lækjargata 8 ☏ 578 3838, 🌐 hradlestin.is.
Mon–Thurs 11am–10pm, Fri 11am–11pm,
Sat & Sun 5–11pm.

Sporting the most un-Icelandic name you could imagine, "Oriental Express Train" boasts that its menu is full of genuine Indian dishes, though its offerings are tempered to the more conservative Icelandic palate. A curry goes for around 2595kr – note that they're not shy of food colourings.

Aalto Bistro Nordic House

Bergsson Mathús

MAP p.47, POCKET MAP C4
Templarasund 3 ☎ 571 1822, ⊕ bergsson
.is. Daily 7am–10pm.

This snug bistro serves home-
made dishes such as spinach
lasagne and chilli con carne
(1590–2290kr). Breakfasts and
brunches featuring the likes of
Spanish ham, eggs, and yoghurt
with muesli and berry jam are
top-notch.

Hannesarholt

MAP p.47, POCKET MAP E6
Grundarstígur 10 ☎ 511 1904. Mon–Fri
8am–5pm, Sat & Sun 11am–5pm; dinner
6.30pm before events.

Former home of Iceland's first
prime minister, Hannes Hafstein,
now a beautifully restored café-
restaurant. The menu is fairly
limited, but excellent cakes and
coffee aside, there's usually fish of
the day, vegetarian pie and a stew
on offer. Weekend events range
from concerts to Icelandic folk
sing-alongs.

Jómfrúin

MAP p.47, POCKET MAP D4
Lækjargata 4 ☎ 551 0100, ⊕ jomfruin.is.
Daily 11am–10pm.

Jómfrúin is a popular Danish-
influenced place specializing in
smørrebrød (open rye sandwiches),
priced at 1900–3500kr. Pick
your toppings from a range
which includes smoked salmon,
caviar, asparagus, smoked eel
and scrambled egg. Fried plaice
(2450kr) is the house speciality.

Skólabrú

MAP p.47, POCKET MAP D4
Pósthússtræti 17 ☎ 511 1690,
⊕ skolabru.is. Daily 5–10pm.

A sophisticated, fine-dining
place offering the likes of seawolf
with roast vegetables served in a
mango, chilli and ginger sauce,
and Parmesan-crusted chicken
with tomatoes and mashed
potatoes. Three-course set menus
start at 6600kr.

Skólabrú

Bars

Ölsmiðjan

MAP p.47, POCKET MAP D4
Lækjargata 10 ☎ 775 6681. Mon–Thurs &
Sun 4pm–1am, Fri & Sat 4pm–5am.

Perhaps not the most sumptuous
of Reykjavík's bars, but then
people come here for the prices,
not the fantastic interior design:
you can get a beer for roughly the
same price charged by other places
during their happy hours. Long
weekend opening hours complete
the deal.

Samtökin 78

MAP p.47, POCKET MAP C4
Suðurgata 3 ☎ 552 7878,
⊕ samtokin78.is. Thurs 8–11pm.

Once a week, Reykjavík's gay
community gathers here at the
new premises of the Icelandic
national LGBT+ association,
Samtökin '78, for an evening of
chat, discussion and the chance to
socialize over a beer or a coffee.
The community centre is also
open to non-Icelanders, and you
can be sure of a warm and friendly
welcome.

Bankastræti and around

Northeast of the National Gallery, Lækjartorg Square is bounded to the east by Bankastræti and by Lækjargata to the south. Lækjargata once marked the eastern boundary of the town and Tjörnin still empties into the sea through a small brook which now runs under the road here (lækjar comes from lækur, meaning "brook") – occasionally, when there's an exceptionally high tide, seawater gushes back along the brook, pouring into Tjörnin. The cluster of old timber buildings up on the small hill immediately south of Bankastræti is known as Bernhöftsstofan and, following extensive renovation, they now house a couple of chichi fish restaurants (see p.58). Named after Tönnies Daniel Bernhöft, a Dane who ran a nearby bakery, they're flanked to the north by one of Iceland's most important buildings, Stjórnarráðshúsið.

Menntaskólinn and Stjórnarráðshúsið

MAP p.54, POCKET MAP D4–D5
Both closed to the public.

Reykjavík's elegant old Grammar School, **Menntaskólinn**, built in 1844, once had to be accessed by a bridge over the brook. It also housed the Alþingi before the completion of the current Alþingishúsið (see p.28) in nearby Austurvöllur Square. Just north of Bankastræti, the small, unobtrusive white building at the foot of Arnahóll hill (see opposite) is, in fact, one of the seats of power in Iceland: **Stjórnarráðshúsið** (Government House) contains the cramped working quarters of the prime minister. It's one of the city's oldest-surviving buildings, built in 1761–71 as a prison.

Menntaskólinn

Arnahóll

MAP p.54, POCKET MAP E3

Up on **Arnahóll**, the grassy mound behind the Icelandic prime minister's offices, a statue of Ingólfur Arnarson, Reykjavík's first settler, surveys his domain; with his back turned on the National Theatre, and the government ministries to his right, he looks out to the ocean that brought him here over eleven centuries ago. Experts believe this is the most likely spot where the pillars of Ingólfur's high seat – a sort of Viking-era throne – finally washed up; according to *Landnámabók*, they were found "by Arnarhvál below the heath".

Arnahóll

Hverfisgata

MAP p.54, POCKET MAP E4–K6

One of central Reykjavík's main thoroughfares, **Hverfisgata** has always played second fiddle to its more glitzy neighbour to the south, Laugavegur. True, it has fewer bars, restaurants and shops than Laugavegur, but a recent makeover has improved things greatly – new pavements have been laid and the whole street has been spruced up. Hverfisgata is at its grandest at its southern end – it's here you'll find the elegant **Danish Embassy** at no. 29 and also the former National Library, now the Safnahús museum, just a few doors down.

Magnússon's manuscripts

Despite so many of Iceland's sagas and histories being written down by medieval monks for purposes of posterity, there existed no suitable means of protecting them from the country's damp climate, and within a few centuries these unique artefacts were rotting away. Enter **Árni Magnússon** (1663–1730), humanist, antiquarian and professor at the University of Copenhagen, who attempted to ensure the preservation of as many of the manuscripts as possible by sending them to Denmark for safekeeping. Although he completed his task in 1720, eight years later many of them went up in flames in the Great Fire of Copenhagen, and Árni died a heartbroken man fifteen months later, never having accepted his failure to rescue the manuscripts, despite braving the flames himself.

In 1961, legislation was passed in Denmark decreeing that manuscripts composed or translated by Icelanders should be returned, but it took a further ruling by the Danish Supreme Court, in March 1971, to get things moving. Finally, however, in April of that year, a Danish naval frigate carried the first texts, Konungsbók Eddukvæða and Flateyjarbók, across the Atlantic into Reykjavík, to be met by crowds bearing signs reading "handritin heim" ("the manuscripts are home") and waving Icelandic flags. A new building, the **Hús íslenskra fræða** (House of Icelandic Studies), is currently under construction near the National Museum on Suðurgata to house the collection.

Bankastræti and around

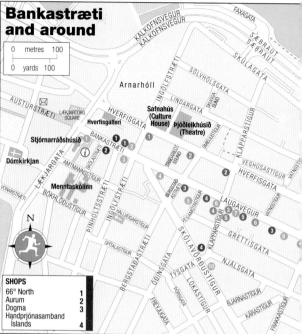

| 0 | metres | 100 |
| 0 | yards | 100 |

SHOPS

66° North	1
Aurum	2
Dogma	3
Handprjónasamband Íslands	4

Safnahús (Culture House)

MAP ABOVE, POCKET MAP E4
Hverfisgata 15 ☎ 530 2210,
☷ culturehouse.is. Tues–Sun
10am–5pm. 1200kr.

Sadly, the **Safnahús** has lost its way. Once the home of a remarkable exhibition about Iceland's medieval manuscripts, today the museum has been subject to an amateurish makeover and contains nothing more than a hotchpotch of seemingly random items from the country's past. While individual pieces may impress, the overriding impression left on the visitor by the muddled exhibition (known as "Points of View") is one of disappointment – this could, and should, be so much better.

Though the **ground floor** is predominantly given over to religious art, it also, confusingly, contains more contemporary items such as a photographic portrait of former Icelandic president, Vigdís Finnbogadóttir, plonked alongside an ornate seventeenth-century tapestry and a sculpture of Mary from the church in Vatnsfjörður, dated around 1400–1500. It's a juxtaposition which doesn't work. Elsewhere on the ground floor, however, do look out for the various versions of *Jónsbók*, a grouping of ancient legal texts which date from 1281; most impressive is the modern copy of a text from 1363, replete with ornately decorated initial letters.

The **first and second floors** contain a mishmash of exhibits – and, once again, the ad hoc combination of items is quite arbitrary: for example, a magnificent altar piece from the church at Grenjaðarstaður, dating from 1766, rubs shoulders with a garish piece of modern art from 1948, *Big sister and little*

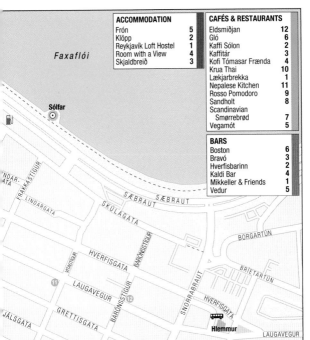

Faxaflói

ACCOMMODATION	
Frón	5
Klöpp	2
Reykjavik Loft Hostel	1
Room with a View	4
Skjaldbreið	3

CAFÉS & RESTAURANTS	
Eldsmiðjan	12
Gló	6
Kaffi Sólon	2
Kaffitár	3
Kofi Tómasar Frænda	4
Krua Thai	10
Lækjarbrekka	1
Nepalese Kitchen	11
Rosso Pomodoro	9
Sandholt	8
Scandinavian Smørrebrød	7
Vegamót	5

BARS	
Boston	6
Bravó	3
Hverfisbarinn	2
Kaldi Bar	4
Mikkeller & Friends	1
Vedur	5

Sólfar

brother by Kristján Davíðsson. That said, it's worth seeking out the stuffed **great auk**, hidden away in a small alcove off the main staircase leading to the top floor. Bought at auction in London in 1971, it's thought the bird was killed at Hólmsberg on the Reykjanes Peninsula (see p.80) – the last two great auks in the world were bludgeoned to death on June 3, 1844 on the nearby island of Eldey.

Laugavegur

MAP ABOVE, POCKET MAP G5–K6

From Lækjartorg, turn right into the short Bankastræti and on, up the small hill, into **Laugavegur** (either "washing road" or "hot spring road"), the route once taken by local washerwomen to the springs in Laugardalur. This is Iceland's major commercial artery, and although it has lost some local business in recent years to nearby shopping malls, it has survived by going upmarket or niche – you'll find many of the stylish domestic outdoor gear stores here, alongside a smattering of arty design shops. There's also a fair number of cafés, bars and restaurants, not to mention the infamous Icelandic Phallological Museum (see p.61), given away by the tourist hordes milling outside. Not surprisingly, therefore, on Friday and Saturday evenings in summer it's bumper to bumper with cars, horns blaring and with well-oiled revellers hanging out of the passenger windows. However, during the summer months, large sections of Laugavegur are accessible only to pedestrians and cyclists – a decision by the City Council that has been warmly welcomed by the majority of the city's population, who have long complained that this was one of the city's worst bottlenecks.

Handprjónsamband Íslands

Shops

66° North

MAP p.54, POCKET MAP E4
Bankastræti 5 ☎ 535 6680, Ⓦ 66north
.com. Daily 9am–10pm.

Renowned for good-quality (if
expensive) clothes which are
guaranteed to keep the worst of
the Icelandic weather at bay –
there's more than a grain of truth
in their slogan: "Keeping Iceland
warm since 1926".

Aurum

MAP p.54, POCKET MAP E4
Bankastræti 4 ☎ 551 2770, Ⓦ aurum.is.
Mon–Fri 10am–6pm, Sat 11am–5pm,
Sun 1–5pm.

Contemporary Nordic design: one
half of the store features very cool
jewellery in silver, lava and gold;
the other side is full of quirky art
pieces for the home. Anyone for a
raven hanging mobile?

Dogma

MAP p.54, POCKET MAP G5
Laugavegur 32 ☎ 562 6600, Ⓦ dogma.is.
Mon–Thurs & Sat 10am–6pm, Fri
10am–6.30pm, Sun 1–6pm.

If you're after a T-shirt as
a souvenir of your stay in
Reykjavík, chances are you'll
find a strong contender here.

They stock the classic *ég tala
ekki íslensku* ("I don't speak
Icelandic") range, among others.

Handprjónasamband
Íslands

MAP p.54, POCKET MAP F5
Skólavörðustígur 19 ☎ 445 5544,
Ⓦ handknit.is. Mon–Sat 10am–6pm,
Sun noon–6pm.

The Icelandic Handknitting
Association sells an astounding
number of home-made woollens.
Each item has been produced by a
knitter in the Reykjavík area, and
quality is high – reckon on around
22,000kr for a decent sweater. Tax-
free shopping available (see p.129).

Cafés

Kaffi Sólon

MAP p.54, POCKET MAP E4
Bankastræti 7a ☎ 562 3232. Mon–Thurs
11am–11.30pm, Fri & Sat 11am–1am,
Sun 11am–11pm.

Decked out in contemporary
Icelandic design, this is one of
Reykjavík's most popular cafés and
serves a good range of light meals
(upwards of 1990kr) – from beef
teriyaki and burgers to deep-fried
camembert and salads – as well as
heartier mains (around 3990kr).

Kaffitár

MAP p.54, POCKET MAP E4
Bankastræti 8 ☎ 420 2732, ⓦ kaffitar
.is. Mon–Sat 7.30am–6pm, Sun 9am–5pm.

The Icelandic version of
Starbucks, but with far better
coffee, made from expertly
blended beans (available as a
brand in supermarkets). The
usual run of cakes and muffins
is on offer, too, plus good
croissants.

Kofi Tómasar Frænda

MAP p.54, POCKET MAP E4
Laugavegur 2 ☎ 551 1855. Mon–Thurs
11am–1am, Fri & Sat 10am–5am, Sun
10am–midnight.

Also known simply as *Kofinn*,
trendy young Reykjavíkers flock
to this chilled place to loll around
on the comfortable couches,
chat, drink coffee and work on
their poetry. Its prime position
on Laugavegur is also great for
people-watching.

Sandholt

MAP p.54, POCKET MAP G5
Laugavegur 36 ☎ 551 3524, ⓦ sandholt
.is. Daily 7am–9pm.

The best café-cum-bakery in town
with good coffee and excellent
strawberry tarts, cinnamon

Gló

Kaffi Sólon

swirls, flans, fresh sandwiches
and handmade chocolates. Also
serves breakfast including fresh
croissants, muesli and *skyr*.

Restaurants

Eldsmiðjan

MAP p.54, POCKET MAP J6
Laugavegur 81 ☎ 562 3838, ⓦ eldsmidjan
.is. Daily 11am–11pm.

Boasting a prime location on the
main drag, *Eldsmiðjan* serves the
best pizzas in Reykjavík, made
in an oven that burns Icelandic
birchwood. There's also a takeaway
service available. A twelve-incher
starts at 3495kr.

Gló

MAP p.54, POCKET MAP F5
Laugavegur 20B ☎ 553 1111, ⓦ glo.is.
Daily 11am–10pm.

Unusually decorated with slices
of birch trunks, this popular
vegetarian place serves up the
likes of parsley root soup with
hummus (1250kr) and nut stew
(1990kr). The emphasis is very
much on fresh produce, with
much of it served uncooked.
Also sells a wide range of fresh,
tasty juices.

Lækjarbrekka

Krua Thai

MAP p.54, POCKET MAP F6
Skólavörðustíg 21a ☎ 552 2525,
ⓦ kruathai.is. Mon–Fri 11.30am–9.30pm,
Sat noon–9.30pm, Sun 5–9.30pm.
This cosy, no-nonsense Thai place
offers exceptional value, with a
huge choice of single-dish meals
– green curry, pad thai and the
like – for around 2100kr. Servings
are generous and prices include
rice. At lunchtime, a portion of
three different set dishes with rice
goes for a mere 1590kr.

Lækjarbrekka

MAP p.54, POCKET MAP D4
Bankastræti 2 ☎ 551 4430,
ⓦ laekjarbrekka.is. Daily 11.30am–11pm.
Housed in an old wooden
building with period furnishings,
Lækjarbrekka offers a refined
atmosphere and fabulous seafood
– including lunchtme set menus
(3690kr). The "Icelandic taste"
(2450kr) includes fermented
shark, gravlax and dried cod; also
superb langoustine soup and *skyr*
mousse with blueberry sorbet.

Nepalese Kitchen

MAP p.54, POCKET MAP H6
Laugavegur 60A ☎ 517 7795,
ⓦ nepalesekitchen.is. Tues–Sun
11am–11pm.
This Nepalese restaurant has a
deserved reputation for serving
some seriously tasty dishes from
the Indian subcontinent: mains,
such as Nepalese chicken masala
and any number of lamb and
vegetarian specialities, start at
around 3010kr. You can get a
fifteen percent discount if you're
ordering takeaway.

Rosso Pomodoro

MAP p.54, POCKET MAP G5
Laugavegur 40 ☎ 561 0500,
ⓦ rossopomodoro.is. Mon–Thurs
11.30am–10pm, Fri & Sat 11.30am–11pm,
Sun 5–10pm.
A genuinely good southern
Italian restaurant, drawing
inspiration from Neapolitan
cuisine. Pizzas and pasta dishes
go for around 3200kr, salads start
at 1790kr and grilled chicken
with Parma ham, mozzarella and
red wine sauce, for example, is
4490kr.

Scandinavian Smørrebrød

MAP p.54, POCKET MAP F5
Laugavegur 22A ☎ 578 4888,
ⓦ scandinavian.is. Mon–Thurs & Sun
noon–10pm, Fri & Sat noon–11pm.
Despite the name, this place
serves mainly Icelandic rather
than Scandinavian specialities,
such as reindeer pâté, lobster
soup and various lamb dishes
(mains around 3500kr). They
also serve up pasta, burgers, and
a range of open sandwiches.

Vegamót

MAP p.54, POCKET MAP F5
Vegamótastígur 4 ☏ 511 3040,
ⓦ vegamot.is. Kitchen Mon–Thurs & Sun
11am–10pm, Fri & Sat 11am–11pm.

A favourite hangout for
Reykjavík's trendy young things,
who come here for the good-value
burgers (2790kr), salads (2690kr),
Mexican specials (2790kr), and
the excellent weekend brunch (Sat
& Sun 11am–4pm; from 2590kr).

Bars

Boston

MAP p.54, POCKET MAP G5
Laugavegur 28B ☏ 571 5781. Mon–Thurs &
Sun 2pm–1am, Fri & Sat 2pm–3am.

Crowded, bohemian bar known
for its laidback atmosphere. DJs
or live music sets Thurs–Sat.

Bravó

MAP p.54, POCKET MAP F5
Laugavegur 22 ☏ 823 7892. Mon–Thurs &
Sun 7pm–1am, Fri & Sat 7pm–4.30am.

In various guises, this spot has
been one of Reykjavík's most
popular bars for years, and is a
great place to start the evening.
The music policy is varied,
embracing everything from
electro to indie and classic hits.

Mikkeller & Friends

Hverfisbarinn

MAP p.54, POCKET MAP F4
Hverfisgata 20 ☏ 571 3990. Fri & Sat
9pm–3am.

The bar and club here on the
corner of Hverfisgata and
Smiðjustígur has always been
popular with Reykjavík's in-
crowd. Hverfisbarinn is now back
in business after a makeover and
is still attracting anyone who's
young and beautiful – or at least
who thinks they are. There are
often long queues to get in.

Kaldi Bar

MAP p.54, POCKET MAP F5
Laugavegur 20B ☏ 581 2200, ⓦ kaldibar
.com. Mon–Thurs & Sun noon–1am, Fri &
Sat noon–3am.

Kaldi Bar serves up any
number of beers from the Kaldi
microbrewery in Árskógssandur,
near Akureyri. They play low
background music, so if you're
looking for a place to chat over a
drink, it's a sound choice. Note,
though, that it's usually pretty
packed.

Mikkeller & Friends

MAP p.54, POCKET MAP E4
Hverfisgata 12 ☏ 437 0203,
ⓦ mikkeller.dk/location/mikkeller-
friends-reykjavik. Mon–Thurs & Sun
5pm–1am, Fri & Sat 2pm–1am.

With twenty beers on tap, all
from microbreweries, this great
little top-floor bar is a beer
drinker's heaven. It's cosy and
snug inside, and a really good
place to kick the evening off with
a drink or two.

Vedur

MAP p.54, POCKET MAP F5
Klapparstígur 33 ⓦ verdurbarinn.is.
Daily noon–1am.

Very relaxed and friendly place
whose eccentric Spanish manager
mixes magnificent cocktails and
serves up free tapas while you sit
sipping at the bar. A great spot to
chill. Gets some custom from the
gay bar next door.

Hallgrímskirkja and around

From the western end of Laugavegur, Skólavörðustígur streaks steeply upwards to the largest church in the country, the magnificent Hallgrímskirkja, a magnet for all tourists visiting Reykjavík. With its burgeoning number of shops and restaurants, the street is fast becoming a rival to Laugavegur, albeit in shorter form. Thanks to its hilltop vantage point, meanwhile, the church enjoys some of the best views of central Reykjavík of anywhere in the city. From Hallgrímskirkja, it's an easy stroll back down the hill, perhaps detouring via the excellent swimming pool, Sundhöllin (see p.125), towards Hlemmur, Reykjavík's main bus interchange, and on to the seafront. Here, there are sweeping views out over Faxaflói bay across to Mount Esja in the distance.

Hallgrímskirkja

MAP p.62, POCKET MAP G7
Skólavörðuholt ☎ 510 1000,
Ⓦ hallgrimskirkja.is. Daily: May–Sept
9am–9pm; Oct–Apr 9am–5pm. Free;
viewing platform 900kr.

The Reykjavík skyline is dominated by this modern concrete structure, with its neatly composed, space-shuttle-like form. Work began on the church – named after the renowned seventeenth-century religious poet Hallgrímur Pétursson – immediately after World War II, but was only completed in 1986, the slow progress due to the task being carried out by a family firm comprising one man and his son. The work of state architect Guðjón Samúelsson, the church's unusual design – not least its 73m steeple – has divided the city over the years, although locals have grown to accept rather than love it since its consecration. Most people rave about the **pipe organ** inside, the only decoration in an otherwise completely bare, Gothic-style shell; measuring a whopping 15m in height and possessing over five thousand pipes, it really

has to be heard (during services) to be believed.

The tower has a **viewing platform**, accessed by a lift from just within the main door, giving stunning panoramic views across Reykjavík; note that it's open to the elements.

Leifur Eiríksson statue

MAP p.62, POCKET MAP G7
With his back to the church and his gaze firmly planted on

Hallgrímskirkja

Time is of the essence

Spend any time in Reykjavík and you'll soon understand that the city lives at the mercy of the elements. Rain and snow storms can appear as if from nowhere and howling winds, tearing straight in off the sea, can cut through all but the most robust of outdoor gear. Understand that and it's easy to see why no two public clocks in Reykjavík tell the same time. Exposure to the sea, altitude and general meteorological mayhem cause radically diverse wind conditions in different parts of the city. At the top of Hallgrímskirkja tower, for example, the wind is so strong that the hands on the clock are frequently blown off course. It's something Icelanders don't give a second thought to, of course, but it's not unusual to spot baffled tourists double-checking their watches to make sure of the correct time.

Vínland, the imposing statue of **Leifur Eiríksson**, the Icelandic explorer who is considered by many to have discovered North America, was donated by the US in 1930 to mark the Icelandic parliament's thousandth birthday. This is one of the highest parts of Reykjavík, and on a clear day there are great **views** out over the surrounding houses adorned with multicoloured corrugated-iron facades.

Einar Jónsson Museum

MAP p.62, POCKET MAP F7
Eiríksgata 3 ☎ 551 3797, ⓦ lej.is.
Tues–Sun 10am–5pm. 1000kr.

The heroic form of Leifur Eiríksson is found in several other statues around the city, many of them the work of **Einar Jónsson** (1874–1954), who is remembered by this museum, housed in a pebble-dash building to the right of Hallgrímskirkja. Einar lived here in an increasingly reclusive manner until his death in 1954; a specially constructed group of rooms, connected by slim corridors and a spiral staircase, takes the visitor through a chronological survey of Einar's career. His style of sculpture varies widely, though is often influenced by his spiritual beliefs and by Icelandic mythology. If

the museum is closed, peek into the **garden** at the rear, where there are several examples of Einar's work on display; his most visible work, the statue of independence leader Jón Sigurðsson, stands in front of the Alþingishúsið (see p.28).

Phallological Museum

MAP p.62, POCKET MAP K6
Laugavegur 116 ☎ 561 6663, ⓦ phallus.is.
Daily 10am–6pm. 1500kr.

The **Phallological Museum** is easy to spot – just look for the bemused-looking tourists standing outside, not quite believing that this is, indeed, a museum dedicated to the penis. Visitors can ogle the members of around three hundred mammals, displayed in jars of formaldehyde and alcohol. It's now possible to size up a human specimen too, following the death of 95-year-old Páll Arason, who had pledged his manhood to the museum (be warned – it comes complete with long white wisps of pubic hair). And there's more: a misshapen foreskin removed in an emergency operation and a pair of human testicles are also on display. After that, you'll no doubt be ready for the plaster cast and photos of several former museum visitors, which leave little to the imagination.

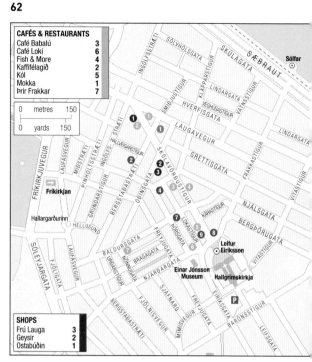

CAFÉS & RESTAURANTS	
Café Babalú	3
Café Loki	6
Fish & More	4
Kaffifélagið	2
Kól	5
Mokka	1
Þrír Frakkar	7

SHOPS	
Frú Lauga	3
Geysir	2
Ostabúðin	1

Sólfar

MAP ABOVE, POCKET MAP H4
Sæbraut.

Down on Sæbraut, the main road which runs along Reykjavík's shoreline, sits the strikingly modern-looking sculpture **Sólfar**

("Sun Voyager"). Designed in shiny steel by the artist Jón Gunnar Árnason (1931–89), it depicts a stylised Viking longship, complete with crew and oars, sailing out north across the bay towards distant mountains – though Árnason himself stated that it was

Sólfar

Hallgrímskirkja and around

Faxaflói

Höfði

BARS	
Björgarðurinn	2
Hlemmur Square	3
Kaffibarinn	1

ACCOMMODATION	
Adam	9
Fosshótel Baron	1
Fosshótel Lind	10
Fosshótel Reykjavík	3
Guesthouse 101	5
Hlemmur Square	6
Leifur Eiriksson	8
Luna	7
Óðinsvé	4
Reykjavik4you Apartment Hotel	2

intended to depict a dream vessel floating off to new beginnings, and wanted it to face westwards, towards the setting sun. Either way it's an elegant piece, fast becoming one of the most photographed of Reykjavík's attractions.

Höfði

MAP ABOVE, POCKET MAP P2
Borgartún. Closed to the public.
East of Sólfar, it's a five-minute stroll back along Sæbraut to **Höfði**, a stocky white wooden structure built in 1909 in Jungendstil, which occupies a grassy square beside the shore, between Sæbraut and Borgartún. Originally home to the French consul, the house also played host to Winston Churchill in 1941 when he visited British forces stationed in Iceland. Although Höfði is best known as the location for the 1986 snap summit between Soviet President Mikhail

Gorbachev and US President Ronald Reagan, Icelanders know it equally well for its resident ghost, said to be that of a young girl who poisoned herself after being found guilty of incest with her brother.

Höfði

Shops

Frú Lauga

MAP p.62, POCKET MAP F5
Óðinsgata 1 ☎ 534 7165, ⓦ frulauga.is.
Mon–Fri 11am–6pm , Sat 11am–4pm.
Farmers' market selling the
freshest of Icelandic fruit and
vegetables – from raspberries to
broccoli – delivered directly to
the shop every day from across
the country.

Geysir

MAP p.62, POCKET MAP F5
Skólavörðustígur 16 ☎ 519 6000,
ⓦ geysir.com. Daily 10am–10pm.
This is the only place you should
consider buying a pure wool
Icelandic blanket – even though
you'll need to part with around
30,000kr. The quality is far
superior to other shops and tax-
free shopping is available.

Ostabúðin

MAP p.62, POCKET MAP E5
Skólavörðustígur 8 ☎ 562 2272,
ⓦ ostabudin.is. Mon–Thurs 10am–6pm,
Fri 10am–6.30pm, Sat 11am–4pm.
Ostabúðin offers a great
choice of Icelandic cheeses, as
well as charcuterie and other
delicatessen items. Downstairs

Geysir

there are also a few tables where
you can get a light lunch – try the
creamy fish soup.

Cafés and restaurants

Café Babalú

MAP p.62, POCKET MAP F6
Skólavörðustígur 22a ☎ 555 8845,
ⓦ babalu.is. Daily 11am–11pm.
This quirky, bohemian café
occupies two floors of a brightly
painted yellow building and is
popular with an alternative crowd.
Their cheesecake is heavenly.

Café Loki

MAP p.62, POCKET MAP F7
Lokastígur 28 ☎ 466 2828, ⓦ loki.is.
Mon–Sat 9am–9pm, Sun 11am–9pm.
Traditional Icelandic food at
reasonable prices: meat soup
(1850kr), herring plate (2400kr),
sheep head jelly on flatbread
(1840kr) and *skyr* (820kr). Great
views of Hallgrímskirkja from
upstairs.

Fish & More

MAP p.62, POCKET MAP F6
Skólavörðustígur 23 ☎ 571 1289.
Daily 8am–10pm.
Instead of battering and frying,
this fish restaurant steams the
catch and serves it with veggies
(2290kr); check the blackboard
to see what's fresh in that day.
There's often a deliciously tangy
fish soup, too (1890kr).

Kaffifélagið

MAP p.62, POCKET MAP E5
Skólavörðustígur 10 ☎ 520 8420,
ⓦ kaffifelagid.is. Mon–Fri 10.30am–6pm,
Sat 10am–4pm.
Proudly boasting to be the
smallest café in the whole of
Iceland, this minuscule place
serves a range of different coffees
produced by the Italian company,
Ottolina, which has been in
operation since 1947. Either

Kaffifélagið

bistro with definite leanings towards traditional Icelandic game: horse tenderloin with mushrooms (6250kr), *plokkfiskur* (fish and potato mash; 3900kr) and smoked guillemot (5690kr).

drink in or take away; ground coffee beans are also available for purchase.

Kól

MAP p.62, POCKET MAP F6
Skólavörðustígur 40 ☎ 517 7474,
Ⓦ kolrestaurant.is. Lunch Mon–Fri 11.30am–2pm; dinner Mon–Thurs & Sun 5.30–10pm, Fri 5.30–11pm.

This classy place is named after the *kól* (charcoal) over which they cook their meat: the grilled lamb sirloin with polenta, carrots and goat's cheese, for example, is delicious (5790kr). The fish – from charred salmon to plaice – is also tasty.

Mokka

MAP p.62, POCKET MAP E5
Skólavörðustígur 3a ☎ 552 1174.
Daily 9am–6.30pm.

Reykjavík's oldest café opened in 1958, and was the first in the country to serve espresso and cappuccino to its curious clientele. A changing display of photographs adorn the walls, and there's a no-music policy.

Þrir Frakkar

MAP p.62, POCKET MAP E7
Baldursgata 14 ☎ 552 3939,
Ⓦ 3frakkar.com. Mon–Fri noon–2.30pm & 6–10pm, Sat & Sun 6–10pm.

Strange name ("Three Overcoats") for this backstreet, French-style

Bars

Bjórgarðurinn

MAP p.62, POCKET MAP P2
Þórunnartún 1 ☎ 531 9030,
Ⓦ bjorgardurinn.is. Daily 4pm–midnight.

Attached to the *Fosshótel*, the "Beer Garden" has an impressive range of beer both on tap and in bottles, including pilsner, stout, pale ale and brown ale. Happy hour is 4–7pm, when there are some great deals to be had. Don't miss the sausages in a brioche bun, either.

Hlemmur Square

MAP p.62, POCKET MAP K6
Laugavegur 105 ☎ 415 1600,
Ⓦ www.hlemmursquare.com/bistro-bar.
Daily 3–10pm.

The trendy bar inside the *Hlemmur Square* hostel (see p.115) should be your number one choice for happy hour (4–8pm), with beers priced at an amazing 600kr (there are several Icelandic ones on tap, as well as Tuborg), and even cocktails going for just 1000kr.

Kaffibarinn

MAP p.62, POCKET MAP F5
Bergstaðastræti 1 ☎ 551 1588. Mon–Thurs & Sun 5pm–1am, Fri & Sat 3pm–5am.

With an unmistakable red corrugated-iron frontage emblazoned with the famous London underground logo, this tiny bar fancies itself as an arty hangout and trades on the rumour that Blur's Damon Albarn owns it, however unlikely. Be that as it may, it's still perhaps your best bet for a great night out in Reykjavík and is a legend on the scene.

Öskjuhlíð and around

The wooded hill of Öskjuhlíð (60m above sea level) affords spectacular views of the city, and is a popular recreation area for Reykjavíkers, who flock here to explore the paths that crisscross its verdant slopes. Öskjuhlíð has, in fact, only been wooded since 1950, when a forestation programme began after soil erosion had left it barren and desolate. A plot of land on the hill's southern side, near the inlet of Fossvogur and the Fossvogskirkjugarður cemetery, has recently been earmarked as the location for a temple to the Æsir, the heathen gods of Viking times, though building work seems to have stalled temporarily.

Perlan

MAP OPPOSITE, POCKET MAP N4
Öskjuhlíð ☏ 562 0200. Daily 10am–9pm.
Free.

If you arrive in Reykjavík from Keflavík airport, it's hard to miss the space-age-looking grey

Perlan

container tanks that sit at the top of the wooded hill, Öskjuhlíð. Each is capable of holding four thousand litres of water at 80°C for use in the capital's homes, offices and swimming pools; it's also from here that water has traditionally been pumped, via a network of specially constructed pipes, underneath Reykjavík's pavements to keep them ice- and snow-free during winter. **Perlan**'s name – The Pearl – comes from its glittering, glassy dome, which sits on top of the tanks and can be seen from miles away.

Being on top of a hill, the dome itself offers excellent 360-degree **panoramic views** of the entire city: simply take the lift to the fourth floor and step outside. On a clear day you can see all the way to the Snæfellsjökull glacier at the tip of the Snæfellsnes peninsula, as well as the entirety of Reykjavík. Before leaving, make sure you see the artificial indoor **geyser simulator** that erupts every few minutes from the basement, shooting a powerful jet of water all the way to the fourth floor: it's a good taste of what's to come if you're heading out to the real thing at Geysir (see p.90).

Öskjuhlíð and around

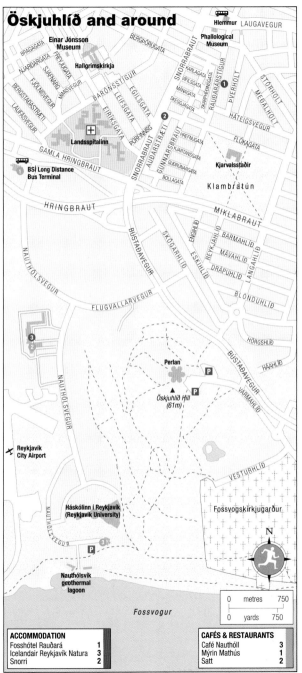

ACCOMMODATION

Fosshótel Rauðará	1
Icelandair Reykjavík Natura	3
Snorri	2

CAFÉS & RESTAURANTS

Café Nauthóll	3
Mýrin Mathús	1
Satt	2

Nauthólsvík geothermal lagoon

MAP p.67, POCKET MAP N4
Nauthólsvegur ☎ 551 3177, ⓦ nautholsvik
.is. Mid-May to mid-Aug daily 10am–7pm;
rest of year Mon & Wed 11am–2pm &
5–8pm, Fri 11am–2pm, Sat 11am–4pm.
Mid-May to mid-Aug free, rest of year
600kr.

At the southern end of Öskjuhlíð, close to the Reykjavík Sailing Club, there's an artificial beach of bright yellow sand, known as Ylströnd, where it's possible to swim in an enclosed **seawater lagoon** (the water temperature is generally 15–19°C). There are also two hot pots on the beach (around 38°C), one of which is built into the sand. In the winter, the temperature in the lagoon is a more invigorating 4-6°C.

Nauthólsvík is one of the best places in the city to relax and take the alfresco waters. Not only does the site offer great views of the southern coastline, but it's also unfenced and open to the surrounding country-side, meaning you can simply come and go as you please. Note that there are no lockers in the changing rooms themselves, just open baskets for your clothes, though it is possible to store

Nauthólsvík geothermal lagoon

valuables for 300kr – ask at the service centre. Remember, as at other Icelandic pools, you must thoroughly shower naked, without a swimming costume, before entering the hot pots.

Kjarvalsstaðir

MAP p.67, POCKET MAP N3
Flókagata 24 ☎ 517 1290, ⓦ artmuseum
.is. Daily 10am–5pm. 1600kr.

Its surroundings of birch trees and pleasant grassy expanses cannot hide the fact that the **Kjarvalsstaðir** art gallery is an ugly 1960s-style concrete structure – even if the interior is surprisingly bright and airy. Part of the Reykjavík Art Museum, Kjarvalsstaðir is devoted to the work of Iceland's most celebrated artist, Jóhannes Sveinsson Kjarval (1885–1972). After working on a fishing trawler during his youth, Jóhannes moved abroad to study art, spending time in London, Copenhagen, France and Italy, but it was only after his return to Iceland in 1940 that he travelled widely in his own country, drawing on the raw beauty he saw around him for the quasi-abstract depictions of Icelandic landscapes which made him one of the country's most popular twentieth-century painters. Painted in oils, much of his work is a surreal fusion of colour: his bizarre yet pleasing *Krítik* ("Critique") from 1946–47, a melee of icy blues, whites and greys measuring a whopping 4m in length and 2m in height, is the centrepiece of the exhibition, portraying a naked man jauntily bending over to expose his testicles while catching a fish, watched over, rather oddly, by a number of Norse warriors. The museum is divided into two halls – the east one shows Jóhannes's work, while the west hall is dedicated to touring temporary exhibitions.

Kjarvalsstaðir

Cafés and restaurants

Café Nauthóll

MAP p.67, POCKET MAP N4
Nauthólsvegur 106 ☎ 599 6660,
Ⓦ nautholl.is. Daily 11am–10pm.

This classy, airy bistro has large windows overlooking Fossvogur bay and serves a good selection of tapas-style nibbles during the day and more substantial mains after 5pm. Also does a tempting weekend brunch (3150kr).

Café Nauthóll

Mýrin Mathús

MAP p.67, POCKET MAP N3
Inside the BSÍ bus terminal,
Vatnsmýrarvegur 10 ☎ 552 1288,
Ⓦ myrinmathus.is. Daily 6am–11pm.

This keenly priced cafeteria inside the BSÍ bus station – whose odd name means something like "Restaurant in the Bog" – is more agreeable than you might expect, serving a selection of burgers and hot dogs, as well as traditional Icelandic dishes. Don't miss their *svið*, boiled sheep's head (served with mashed potato) – and don't be put off by how it looks.

Satt

MAP p.67, POCKET MAP N3
Inside Icelandair Hótel Natura,
Nauthólsvegur 52 ☎ 444 4050,
Ⓦ sattrestaurant.com. Daily
11.30am–10pm.

Complete with a terrace for sunny days, *Satt*, at the *Icelandair Natura* hotel (see p.116), offers a good-value weekday lunch buffet (11.30am–2pm), and a weekend brunch deal (same times). The rest of their menu is a little steep for what you get – burgers for 2750kr, fish & chips for 3350kr – but you're paying for the smart-casual setting.

Eastern Reykjavík

After rambling through central Reykjavík for a good couple of kilometres, Laugavegur comes to an end at the junction with the main north–south artery, Kringlumýrarbraut. Beyond here, Suðurlandsbraut marks the southern reaches of Laugardalur valley, hemmed in between the low hills of Grensás to the south and the northerly Laugarás, just behind Sundahöfn harbour, whose Þvottalaugarnar springs have been known since the time of the Settlement as a source of hot water for washing. The springs are still here, the spot commemorated by the Ásmundur Sveinsson statue, Þvottakonan (The Washerwoman), while the area is also home to Iceland's premier sports ground; an indoor sporting and concert venue; the HI youth hostel and campsite; and the country's largest swimming pool.

Laugardalsvöllur and Laugardalshöll

MAP OPPOSITE, POCKET MAP Q2

Open-air **Laugardalsvöllur** is the country's main sports stadium, hosting all of Iceland's international football and athletics fixtures. The largest attendance here was in 2004 for a friendly football match between Iceland and Italy, when over twenty thousand people packed into the ground to see the game – a staggering seven percent of the entire Icelandic population. Just to the south, across Engjavegur, **Laugardalshöll** hosts international indoor sporting events such as handball, volleyball and basketball. It is also the country's biggest concert venue, holding up to eleven thousand people. Should Iceland ever manage to win the Eurovision Song Contest (the dream of all Icelanders), Laugardalshöll would

Swimming etiquette in Iceland

One of the best things about a trip to Reykjavík is the chance to swim outdoors in the city's geothermally heated swimming pools, whose water usually hovers around 23–25°C, and to loll in divinely warm **hot pots**, which tend to vary between 35 and 39°C. Since water in both the pools and the hot pots doesn't contain chlorine, strict rules are in place to ensure that bathers do not contaminate the water. Firstly, you must leave your outdoor shoes on the racks provided at the entrance to the changing room. Then, having undressed, you must **shower naked**, without a swimming costume, washing your body thoroughly with the soap provided in the areas marked on the multilingual signs posted up in the shower rooms: feet, hair, underarms, groin and bottom. Duty attendants will not hesitate to berate you should they spot you breaking the rules. Squeaky clean, you can now enjoy Iceland's best natural resource.

Eastern Reykjavík

ACCOMMODATION
Arctic Comfort	6
Cabin	1
Grand Reykjavík	3
Hilton Reykjavík Nordica	4
Ísland	5
Kríunes	7
Reykjavík Campsite	2

SHOPS
Eymundsson	1
Finnska Búðin	1
Vínbúðin	1

CAFÉS & RESTAURANTS
Bæjarins Beztu Pylsur	1
Café Blue	1
Hraðlestin	1
Íslenska Hamborgarafabrikkan	1
Joe and the Juice	1
Kaffitár	1

be the most likely choice of venue; Iceland came second in both 1999 and 2009.

Laugardalslaug

MAP ABOVE, POCKET MAP Q2
Sundlaugavegur ⊕ 411 5100, ⊛ itr.is.
Mon–Fri 6.30am–10pm, Sat & Sun 8am–10pm. Entry 950kr.

Laugardalslaug

Since opening in 1968, the swimming complex **Laugardalslaug** has become a Reykjavík institution. It is the biggest in Iceland and features a 50m outdoor pool, a smaller children's pool and paddling pool, two waterslides, numerous hot pots, a steam sauna, gym and mini-golf.

Ásmundarsafn

MAP p.71, POCKET MAP Q2

Sigtún ⓦ artmuseum.is. Daily: May–Sept 10am–5pm; Oct–April 1–5pm. 1600kr.

If sculpture is your thing, you'll want to check out the domed **Ásmundursafn**, dedicated to the work of **Ásmundur Sveinsson** and part of the Reykjavík Art Museum. Sveinsson (1893–1982) was one of the pioneers of Icelandic sculpture, and his powerful, often provocative, work was inspired by his country's nature and literature. During the 1920s he studied in both Stockholm and Paris, returning to Iceland to develop his unique **sculptural Cubism**, a style infused with Icelandic myth and legend. You can view his work here at his former home, which he designed and built with his own hands between 1942 and 1950; he lived where the museum shop and reception are currently located.

The building is an uncommon shape for Reykjavík because, when Ásmundur planned it, he was experimenting with Mediterranean and North African themes, drawing particular inspiration from the domed houses common to Greece. The crescent-shaped building beyond the reception area contains examples of the sculptor's work, including several busts from his period of Greek influence. Note that the original of his most famous sculpture – 1926's **Sæmundur á selnum** (*Sæmundur on the Seal*), which shows one of the first Icelanders to receive a university education, the priest and historian Sæmundur Sigfússon (1056–1133), sitting astride a seal, psalter in hand – is not on display here; it stands outside the main university building on Suðurgata. You will, however, find a smaller version of the original in the museum grounds, where there are also lots of Ásmundur's other soft-edged, gently curved monuments to the ordinary working people of the country.

Botanical Garden

MAP p.71, POCKET MAP Q3

Daily: May–Sept 10am–10pm; Oct–April 10am–3pm. Free.

The green expanses beyond the sports ground (Laugardalshöll) contain the country's most impressive **Botanical Garden**. Barely ten minutes on foot from the Ásmundur Sveinsson sculpture museum, reached by walking east along Engjavegur, the botanical garden contains an extensive collection of native Icelandic flora, as well as thousands of imported plants and trees. This place is particularly popular with Icelandic families, who come here not only to enjoy the surroundings but also for the adjoining family park and small zoo (see opposite), which are a hit with children.

Botanical garden

Húsdýragarðurinn and Fjölskyldugarðurinn

MAP p.71, POCKET MAP Q3
Hafrafell ⓦ mu.is. Daily: June–Aug 10am–6pm; Sept–May 10am–5pm. 860kr. Buses #2, #15 and #17 run from the city centre; get off at the Laugardalshöll stop.

Especially with children in tow, **Husdýragarðurinn zoo** – home to Icelandic mammals such as seals, foxes, mink and reindeer, plus a few farm animals – makes for a thoroughly pleasant afternoon's visit. There's also a collection of fish caught in local rivers and lakes, which will keep younger visitors entertained. Once the attraction of the animals starts to wane, you can check out the surrounding **Fjölskyldugarðurin family park**, where there's a small duck lake complete with replica Viking longboat, a go-kart track, and other activities based loosely on a Viking theme, including a fort and an outlaw hideout.

Kringlan shopping centre

MAP p.71, POCKET MAP P3
Kringlan 4–12 ☏ 517 9000, ⓦ kringlan .is. Mon–Wed 10am–6.30pm, Thurs 10am–9pm, Fri 10am–7pm, Sat 10am–6pm, Sun 1–6pm. A free shuttle bus operates here from outside the tourist office in Aðalstræti, where you'll find departure times. Alternatively, city buses #1, #3, #4 and #6 all come here.

The construction in 1987 of **Kringlan shopping centre** – the biggest in Reykjavík, with some 170 stores – took place amid concerns that it would lead to the closure of many shops in the city centre. Those fears turned out to be unfounded, as both Kringlan and the city centre have experienced an unprecedented boom in recent years, which shows no signs of ending. In addition to its many stores – which are expensive but eature well-known international names such as Diesel, Boss and

Árbæjarsafn

Timberland as well as home-grown outlets – Kringlan also boasts a library, theatre, cinema and a branch of the state-owned alcohol monopoly, *vínbúðin*.

Árbæjarsafn

MAP p.71, POCKET MAP T2
Kistuhylur 4 ☏ 411 6300, ⓦ arbaejarsafn .is. June–Aug daily 10am–5pm. 1400kr.
The **Árbæjarsafn** open-air museum is a collection of turf-roofed and corrugated-iron buildings on the site of an ancient farm that was first mentioned in the sagas around the mid-1400s. The buildings and their contents record the sweeping changes that occurred as Iceland's economy switched from farming to fishing – the arrival of the fishing trawler in the nineteenth century heralded the beginning of the Icelandic industrial revolution – and Reykjavík's rapid expansion. The pretty **turf church** here, dating from 1842, was carefully moved to its present location from Skagafjörður on the north coast in 1960. Next to it, the farmhouse is dominated by an Ásmundur Sveinsson sculpture, *Woman Churning Milk*, illustrating an all-but-lost way of life.

Viðey

POCKET MAP R1
Ⓦ elding.is/videy.

Reached by a short ferry ride from Sundahöfn harbour east of the city centre, and actually the top of an extinct volcano measuring barely 1.7 square kilometres, the island of **Viðey** has a rich heritage dating back to the time of the Settlement. You can see it from the mainland by taking a ten-minute walk north of the Laugardalur area along Dalbraut, which later mutates into Sundagarður. If you fancy a brisk stroll with views of the ocean and a bit of alfresco art thrown in, this is the place to come.

The Imagine Peace Tower

POCKET MAP R1
Ⓦ imaginepeacetower.com.

To the left of the ferry landing on Viðey, in the opposite direction to the church, the unusual wishing-well structure you can see is the **Imagine Peace Tower**. Conceived in 2007 by Yoko Ono as a beacon to world peace and inscribed with the words "imagine peace" in 24 languages, the structure emits a powerful tower of light every night between October 9 (John Lennon's birthday) and December 8 (the anniversary of his death), illuminating the Reykjavík sky.

Shops

Eymundsson

MAP p.71, POCKET MAP P3
Kringlan shopping centre ☏ 540 2145,
Ⓦ eymundsson.is. Mon–Wed 10am–6.30pm, Thurs 10am–9pm, Fri 10am–7pm, Sat 10am–6pm, Sun 1–6pm.

With a good selection of souvenirs, presents, maps and magazines, as well as coffee-table books about Iceland, Eymundsson is always worth a browse.

Finnska Búðin

MAP p.71, POCKET MAP P3
Kringlan shopping centre ☏ 787 7744,
Ⓦ finnskabudin.is. Mon–Wed 10am–6.30pm, Thurs 10am–9pm, Fri 10am–7pm, Sat 10am–6pm, Sun 1–6pm.

Finland's iconic designers Iittala and Marimekko are just some of the names you'll find inside this store, which sells stylish goods from Iceland's Nordic neighbour. There's an impressive selection of glasses, vases, bowls and fabrics, among other things.

Vínbúðin

MAP p.71, POCKET MAP P3
Kringlan shopping centre ☏ 568 9060,
Ⓦ vinbudin.is. Mon–Thurs & Sat 11am–6pm, Fri 11am–7pm.

Perfectly located for nipping in to buy a bottle of wine while out shopping at Kringlan, this outlet of *vínbúðin* is one of the busiest in the country. Knowledgeable staff are on hand to offer advice if you're looking for a specific tipple to match a meal.

Cafés and restaurants

Bæjarins Beztu Pylsur

MAP p.71, POCKET MAP P3
Kringlan shopping centre ☏ 511 1566,
Ⓦ bbp.is. Mon–Wed 10am–7pm, Thurs 10am–9pm, Fri 10am–8pm, Sat 10am–6pm, Sun noon–6pm.

If you're in the market for a quick dine and dash, this long-standing favourite will hit the spot. *Bæjarins* claim that the combination they offer of hot dogs with a remoulade sauce is Iceland's national dish.

Café Blue

MAP p.71, POCKET MAP P3
Kringlan shopping centre ☏ 588 0300,

ⓦ cafebleu.is. Mon–Wed, Fri & Sat 11am–8pm, Thurs 11am–9pm, Sun noon–8pm.

Bright and breezy place with an extensive menu featuring pizzas (from 2390kr), burgers (from 2590kr), sandwiches, salads, pasta dishes (from 2790kr) and soups as well as a few more substantial dishes such as steaks, grilled lamb, fish and chicken (3000–4000kr).

Hraðlestin

MAP p.71, POCKET MAP P3
Kringlan shopping centre ⓣ 578 3838, ⓦ hradlestin.is. Mon–Wed 11am–6.30pm, Thurs 11am–9pm, Fri 11am–7pm, Sat 11am–6pm, Sun 1–6pm.

Serving a range of Indian food – including, curiously, an Indian vegetarian pizza – this is the place to come if you've tired of Iceland's ubiquitous fish of the day and lamb chops. The carrot soup with ginger is good – though remember that, Indian or not, the dishes are geared towards the conservative Icelandic palate.

Íslenska Hamborgarafabrikkan

MAP p.71, POCKET MAP P3
Kringlan shopping centre ⓣ 575 7575,

ⓦ fabrikkan.is. Mon–Thurs & Sun 11am–10pm, Fri & Sat 11am–11pm.

This popular restaurant has a huge choice of burgers, both beef (cooked medium rare) and chicken, costing 2195–3000kr. Try the delicious "Morthens", with bacon, mushrooms, garlic and Béarnaise sauce (2495kr).

Joe and the Juice

MAP p.71, POCKET MAP P3
Kringlan shopping centre ⓣ 551 5757, ⓦ joeandthejuice.is. Mon–Wed & Sat 10am–6pm, Thurs 10am–9pm, Fri 10am–7pm, Sun noon–6pm.

This enterprising juice bar and café blitzes just about everything – from avocado to ginger – into all manner of delicious concoctions.

Kaffitár

MAP p.71, POCKET MAP P3
Kringlan shopping centre ⓣ 588 0440, ⓦ kaffitar.is. Mon–Wed 9.30am–6.30pm, Thurs 9.30am–9pm, Fri 9.30am–7pm, Sat 9.30am–6pm, Sun 12.30–6pm.

This chain opened in Kringlan in 1994 and is one of Reykjavíkers' favourite coffeehouses. Grab a panini, salad or home-made cake from the café's own bakery – perfect for taking a break from the shopping marathon.

Bæjarins Beztu Pylsur

Hafnarfjörður and around

Set amid an extensive lavafield, Hafnarfjörður, just 10km southwest of the capital, is as big as the centre of Reykjavík, although much more provincial in flavour. It's worth making the 25-minute bus ride out here to sample some real Viking food at the town's Viking village, Fjörukráin, and to learn more about the Icelanders' obsession with elves, dwarves and other spiritual beings – Hafnarfjörður is renowned across Iceland as having the country's greatest concentration of huldufólk ("hidden people").

Hafnarfjörður museum

MAP OPPOSITE, POCKET MAP T2
Vesturgata 8. June–Aug daily 11am–5pm;
Sept–May Sat & Sun 11am–5pm. Free.
A stone's throw from the north end of Strandgata, a block north of the harbour, is **Hafnarfjörður museum**, housed in a wooden warehouse dating from the late 1800s and also known as Pakkhúsið. Inside is a passable if somewhat dull portrayal of Hafnarfjörður's life and times, featuring the likes of a stuffed goat and an old fishing boat.

Sívertsens-Hús

MAP OPPOSITE, POCKET MAP T2
Vesturgata 6. June–Aug daily 11am–5pm;
Sept–May Sat & Sun 11am–5pm. Free.
Next door to Hafnarfjörður museum stands **Sívertsens-**
Hús, the town's oldest building, dating from 1803 and once the residence of local trader, boat builder and man-about-town Bjarni Sívertsen. It's now home to a folk museum, stuffed with how-we-used-to-live paraphernalia from the nineteenth century.

Þríhnjúkahellir

MAP OPPOSITE, POCKET MAP T2
☏ 519 5609, ⓦ insidethevolcano.com.
Tours daily mid-May to Oct; 5–6hr including 40min inside the volcano, 42,000kr including return transport from Reykjavík.
About 20km southeast of Reykjavík, near the Bláfjöll ski area, lies **Þríhnjúkahellir**, an accessible, 4000-year-old subterranean **magma chamber** discovered in the 1970s which is like nowhere else in Iceland.

Hafnarfjörður harbour

Hafnarfjörður and around

Reykjavík (7km)

| 0 | metres | 200 |
| 0 | yards | 200 |

N

ACCOMMODATION

Campsite	2
Helguhús	3
Hótel Víking	4
Lava Hostel	1

CAFÉS & RESTAURANTS

Fjaran	5
Fjörugarðurinn	6
Silfur	3
Súfistinn	1
Tilveran	2
Tuk Tuk Thai	4
Von	7

Þríhnjúkahellir (22km)

There's little to see on the surface except for a small volcanic bump amid a landscape of moss and grass – but the scale below ground becomes clear once you've climbed into a **safety cage** and been lowered by crane into the 120m-deep space. Once you've touched down safely at the bottom, you're allowed to wander cautiously over the rough boulders and stones that carpet the floor of Þríhnjúkahellir's 30m-wide chamber. Be sure to check out the walls, too, which are streaked in different colours left by molten minerals, all twisted and spiked by the forces. Normally a chamber such as this would fill with magma during an eruption and then solidify, but in Þríhnjúkahellir's case the molten rock drained out through tunnels, still visible at the sides of the cave floor.

Note that you should wear warm clothes and tough shoes or boots, as there is a 45-minute walk over rough ground at the beginning and end of the tour, to and from the volcano entrance. The tour ends with hot soup and bus transfer back to Reykjavík.

Þríhnjúkahellir

The hidden people

The street of Strandgata and neighbouring Austurgata in Hafnarfjörður are, according to Icelandic folklore, home to the town's population of **hidden people** – elves, dwarves and other spirits who live in entire families between the rocks that are dotted around the town centre. Apparently, elves are only visible to those with second sight, though a majority of Icelanders are quite prepared to admit they believe in them. In fact, an alarming number of new roads constructed across the country have been subject to minor detours around large rocks after workers attempted to move the boulders only to find that their diggers and earth movers broke down time and again in the process. Should you be keen to try out your second sight, occasional **tours** lasting a couple of hours leave from the tourist office at Strandgata 6 (Tues & Fri 2.30pm; 4500kr; ☎ 694 2785, ◍ alfar.is); they weave their way through Hafnarfjörður, visiting the homes of the *huldufólk*, and are led by guide and storyteller Sigurbjörg Karlsdóttir.

Cafés and restaurants

Fjaran

MAP p.77
Strandgata 55 565 1213,
fjorukrain.is. Daily 6–10.30pm.
This snug, wood-panelled
restaurant in the Viking village is
akin to a British country pub. It
serves the same Viking delicacies
as *Fjörugarðurinn*, but feels more
refined (you'll get real plates
rather than wooden platters).

Fjörugarðurinn

MAP p.77
Strandgata 55 565 1213,
fjorukrain.is. Daily 6–10pm.
Designed to resemble a Viking
longhouse, this atmospheric place,
decked out with candles and heavy
wooden tables, serves a full Viking
dinner (9200kr) of seafood soup,
shark, dried haddock and lamb
shank, all washed down with beer
and Black Death schnapps, and
ending on *skyr* for dessert.

Silfur

MAP p.77
Fjarðargata 13–15 555 6996, silfur
.wix.com/silfur. Mon–Wed 10am–11pm,
Thurs–Sat 10am–1am, Sun 11.30am–10pm.
This airy café in the Fjörður mall
enjoys views over the harbour

Fjörugarðurinn

and serves burgers (from 1690kr),
pasta (2290kr), plus fish and chips
(1890kr).

Súfistinn

MAP p.77
Strandgata 9 565 3740, sufistinn.is.
Mon–Thurs 8.15am–11.30pm, Fri 8am–
11.30pm, Sat 10am–11.30pm, Sun
11am–11.30pm.
Hafnarfjörður's main coffee-
house, with outdoor seating in
good weather. It's also a popular
place for a beer of an evening.

Tilveran

MAP p.77
Linnetstígur 1 565 5250,
tilveranrestaurant.is. Mon–Thurs
11.30am–2pm & 6–9pm, Fri & Sat 6–10pm.
A justifiably popular seafood
restaurant with daily lunch specials
including soup, fish of the day and
coffee for 2490kr; in the evening
it's 2990kr for a succulent fish dish
or 4490kr for meaty options.

Tuk Tuk Thai

MAP p.77
Fjarðargata 19 519 8888, tuktukthai
.is. Mon–Sat 11.30am–9pm, Sun 4–9pm.
Pleasant restaurant serving well-
priced one-dish Thai classics:
tom yam (2090kr), tom kha gai
(1850kr), pad thai (1890kr), green
curry (1990kr) and massaman
curry (2150kr). Their takeaway
packages are good value too.

Von

MAP p.77
Strandgata 75 583 6000, vonmathus
.is.Tues–Fri 11.30am–2pm & 5.30–9pm,
Sat 11.30am–2pm & 5.30–10pm, Sun
11.30am–2pm.
There's a Nordic feel to this smart
but relaxed modern restaurant,
with an emphasis on seasonal
Icelandic ingredients. The menu
is short, usually with a catch of
the day (around 3500kr) and lamb
(4500kr). Perhaps better value are
the set tasting menus (6500kr) and
lunch specials (soup, salad and
catch of the day for 2200kr).

The Reykjanes Peninsula

Southwest of Reykjavík city along the multi-lane Route 41, the Reykjanes Peninsula's rugged, lichen-covered lavafields jut out into the stormy waters of the Atlantic. It would be hard to imagine a wilder place so close to the capital, and yet here amid the seemingly bleak and lonely landscape are some real gems – not least the surreal splash of colour at the Blue Lagoon, Iceland's premier thermal spa. A couple of offbeat museums and a bizarre bridge in the middle of nowhere are worth a look in passing, but most of all it's the rocky, surf-streaked coastline, complete with associated birdlife, which rewards a day spent circuiting the peninsula: don't miss Selatangar's spooky ruins, the great auk monument and seething mud pools at Reykjanestá, nor the teeming bird colonies at Hafnaberg and Krýsuvíkurberg. Key sights such as the Blue Lagoon are easily reached on buses, but elsewhere you'll need your own vehicle or to join a tour.

The Blue Lagoon

MAP OPPOSITE, POCKET MAP S3
Off Route 43 near Grindavík, around 45km from Reykjavík Ⓦ bluelagoon.com. Daily Jan–May & Sept–Dec 10am–8pm, June–Aug 8am–10pm. 6100kr for lagoon; additional packages available; advance booking required.

Forget the crush of tour buses, or the extravagant entry fee: your first sight of the **Blue Lagoon**, with its steaming, milky blue waters pooling amid a wilderness of black lava rubble, will make

The Blue Lagoon

you glad you came to Iceland. Wade out into the shallow water (it's just about deep enough for swimming in places) or relax in the shallows, the heat seeping into your muscles; it's especially atmospheric on cold days, when a thick fog swirls and the waters feel even warmer.

The Blue Lagoon has its origins in local seawater, vaporized at the nearby **Svartsengi geothermal power station** and then fed – at a comfortable 38°C or so – into

The Blue Lagoon

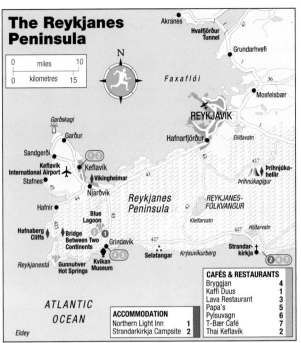

The Reykjanes Peninsula

CAFÉS & RESTAURANTS
Bryggjan 4
Kaffi Duus 1
Lava Restaurant 3
Papa's 5
Pylsuvagn 6
T-Bær Café 7
Thai Keflavík 2

ACCOMMODATION
Northern Light Inn 1
Strandarkirkja Campsite 2

the lagoon. There's also a steam room, plus an artificial waterfall to stand under, while Icelanders scoop handfuls of silvery grey **silt** off the bottom of the lagoon to make facial mudpacks: it's said to cure skin disorders. Whatever the beneficial effects to your skin, your hair will take a real battering from the lagoon's mineral content; rub in plenty of conditioner as protection before bathing.

Vikingheimar (Viking World)

MAP ABOVE, POCKET MAP S2
Víkingabraut 1, Njarðvík; heading west along Route 41, look for the cube-shaped building on the coast, about 5km before Keflavík town ⓦ vikingaheimar.is/en. Feb–Oct 7am–6pm; Nov–Jan check website for hours. 1500kr.

Despite their reputation as fearsome warriors, the Vikings were also great traders and travellers, and the centrepiece of

Vikingheimar is the *Íslendingur*, a full-sized replica **Viking longship**. Before finding a home here, this working model crossed the Atlantic in 2000 to celebrate Leifur Eiríksson's discovery of "Vinland" (America), one thousand years earlier. The clinker-built wooden vessel is broad-beamed and must have been fairly stable, but it would still have taken some nerve to brave an Atlantic crossing without so much as a cabin to shelter under; you can walk around on deck, imagining what being crammed alongside a bunch of seasick freebooters and their livestock must have been like. Aside from the ship, the museum has an account of the brief Viking settlement of Vinland (poor rations and harsh weather eventually drove them back) and some period remains found locally, plus a multimedia exhibition on Viking myths.

Lava tubes

Underneath the Reykjanes Peninsula's grey-green tumble of volcanic rubble is a complex network of **lava tubes**, many of which are unexplored. These tunnels were created when the sides of long, narrow lava flows cooled enough to harden and form an insulating tube around the molten centre, which continued to flow until the tunnel drained. Later eruptions buried the tubes, and they'd be unknown today if cave-ins hadn't revealed their presence. More are being discovered every year, but the current pick includes kilometre-long **Raufarholshellir**, with its weird ice formations; the similarly scaled **Buri Cave**, only found in 2005; spectacular **Þríhnúkagígur** (though this is actually a drained magma chamber; see p.76); and **Leiðarendi**, which is perhaps the least exciting, but also the most accessible. Because of the dangers inherent in exploring the tubes, you should only visit them as part of a tour (9900–42,000kr/person); try ⓦextremeiceland.is or ⓦinsidethevolcano.com.

Hafnaberg Cliffs

MAP p.81, POCKET MAP S3
West off Route 425, about 5km south
of Hafnir village.

Iceland's old roadways were once marked by strings of large **stone cairns** known as "priests" (because, quip locals, they showed the path to salvation without ever taking it themselves). One such row survives on Reykjanes, with its tail-end marking a footpath leading 3km west from a roadside parking bay to the **Hafnaberg Cliffs**; along the way you need to watch out for overly protective greater skuas, which nest in the soft sand hereabouts. The cliffs themselves drop sheer into the sea, packed through the summer with thousands of nesting seabirds. Take care near the crumbly edges.

Bridge Between Two Continents

MAP p.81, POCKET MAP S3
Beside Route 425, about 2km south
from the Hafnaberg car park. Free.

The discrepancy between this structure's rather grand title and its appearance – an unimpressive metal footbridge crossing a small ravine – can't help but raise a smile. The gap that the **Bridge Between Two Continents** spans is supposedly part of the rift system where the North American and Eurasian continental plates are tearing apart. Nonetheless, it's all a bit ludicrous, and the "Welcome to America" and "Welcome to Europe" signs at either end – not to mention the monochrome gravel and black-sand scenery – add to the sense of fun.

Reykjanestá

MAP p.81, POCKET MAP S3
Off Route 425 along a 2km-long good
gravel road signposted "Reykjanesviti".

Reykjanestá is the Reykjanes Peninsula's southwestern extremity, a rocky, storm-battered headland whose geothermal potential is being tapped by **Reykjanesvirkjun**, the shiny 100MW power station that you pass on the way in. There's another thermal outlet nearby at **Gunnuhver hot springs**, a compact mess of boiling mud, hissing vents and clouds of sulphurous steam, which last blew itself apart in

2005 – check out the skeletons of boardwalks still dangling over the void. Traces of older building foundations are evidence of former efforts to establish vegetable hothouses here.

Reykjanestá's main vehicle track ends at a coastal car park, where a tall white **lighthouse** stands slightly inland on a hillock; the original was sited on the grassy coastal headland opposite, but fell into the sea during an earthquake. A solidified lava flow from some ancient eruption forms a low platform above the waves; far out to sea you can just pick out the remote sea stack of **Eldey**, which hosts Europe's largest gannet colony. Eldey also has the sad distinction of being where the last known pair of great auks was bludgeoned to death in 1844; there's a giant **bronze auk** in the Reykjanestá car park as a memorial, its beak pointing seawards.

Kvikan Museum

MAP p.81, POCKET MAP S3
Hafnargata 12a, Grindavík Ⓦ grindavik.is /kvikan. Daily 10am–5pm. 1200kr.
There are three separate exhibitions at **Kvikan**, but two – one on geothermal power, and another about local author and Spanish scholar Guðberg Bergsson – can safely be skipped in favour of **Saltfisksetur Íslands** (Icelandic Saltfish Museum). Even today, with tourism replacing fishing as Iceland's main source of income, the country owes a great deal to the cod: the national **coat of arms** was originally a golden cod, filleted and crowned on a red field, and the Icelandic Nobel Laureate, Halldor Laxnes, wasn't exaggerating when he made the memorable comment, "*Lifið er saltfiskur*" ("life is saltfish"), back in the 1930s. Even so, a lack of timber for boatbuilding meant

that Iceland only really became a fishing nation during the late nineteenth century, after the first modern vessels could be imported, but its success swiftly drew farmers off the land to settle in new coastal settlements around the country.

Today, saltfish still accounts for a good slice of Iceland's export earnings, with most of the product shipped to Spain and West Africa. The Saltfish Museum covers all this history brilliantly in models, dioramas, old photographs and – somehow – the authentic smell of salted cod.

Selatangar

MAP p.81, POCKET MAP T3
12km east of Grindavík on Route 427, then south along short gravel road.
Selatangar was once an important seasonal fishing camp for southwestern Iceland, and though abandoned after better ports with modern vessels became established elsewhere during the nineteenth century, many of the settlement's **stone-block** structures survive among an eerie coastal landscape of grey sand and ancient, disintegrating lava flows. It's reached from the car park along a 200m-long path marked out with driftwood and other bits of flotsam, but you probably won't realize that you've arrived anywhere until you begin to notice small, roofless huts and walled-up recesses – careful investigation will uncover well over a dozen – all half-camouflaged among the volcanic boulders.

Selatangar must have been a tough place to live even in summer, given the pernicious fogs which keep materializing and dispersing along with the coastal breeze. Stories of hauntings by a lonely **ghost** named Tanga-Tómas add to the decidedly spooky atmosphere.

Krýsuvíkurberg

MAP p.81, POCKET MAP T3
22km from Grindavík on Route 427,
then turn south at a signpost marked
"Krýsuvíkurbjarg" along a 4km gravel
road. Be prepared to park the car and
walk in if the road proves impassable.

On a sunny day, the seascapes
from the top of **Krýsuvíkurberg**
– a long, crescent-shaped bay
of cliffs – are fabulous, the blue
waters below contrasting with
a clifftop layer of ochre soil and
green grass. You might be lucky
and see a couple of **puffins** here,
but the main inhabitants at
Krýsuvíkurberg are thousands
of fulmars and kittiwakes, all
of which you can hear long
before you reach the top. The
main headland is topped by
a **triangulation point**, which
makes a great spot to admire
the scenery, from where you can
follow the ridges inland and back
around to the car park along
unmarked tracks.

Strandarkirkja

MAP p.81, POCKET MAP T3
Off the eastern end of Route 427,
about 15km from Þorlákshöfn, via
a short sealed road.

A neat, unassuming weatherboard church painted dove
grey and black, offset by its
warm and colourful interior,
Strandarkirkja – the "**Church on
the Seashore**" – was built around
1900 by grateful fishermen after
they survived a shipwreck off
the local coast. There was once a
busy community here, but today
only the church and a handful of
scattered farm buildings remain;
it's a beautiful spot, though, with
green meadows protected from
the seafront by a high stone wall.
Walk along the shore and you'll
probably see seals and plenty of
eider ducks, but watch out if you
try to stroll through the arctic
tern colony along the approach
road – they can turn nasty if you
get too close.

Cafés and restaurants

Bryggjan

MAP p.81
Miðgarði 2, Grindavík ☎ 426 7100.
Daily 8am–10pm.

This cosy harbour restaurant is full
of maritime memorabilia: sextants,
ships' bells, and even the shell of a
huge spider crab. They do coffee,
waffles and light meals, including
tasty lobster soup with home-
made bread (1800kr). Outdoor
tables for sunny days, too.

Kaffi Duus

MAP p.81
Duusgata 10, Keflavík ☎ 421 7080,
ⓦ duus.is/en. Daily 11am–11pm.

At first glance a straight-forward
place, but it's not just the tandoori
chicken (4200kr) which has an
Asian slant: Indian spices also seep
into the bacon-wrapped monkfish
(4550kr) and battered cod and
chips (3800kr). Pricey, but there are
sea views and generous portions.

Bryggjan

T-Bær Café

Lava Restaurant

MAP p.81

Blue Lagoon ☏ 420 8800, ⊕ bluelagoon
.com. Daily: June–Aug noon–9pm; Sept–
May noon–8.30pm.

Set right against a lava wall with
views out over the lagoon, this
place certainly enjoys a superb
setting. The menu features
"modern Icelandic" cuisine: the
rack of lamb is excellent, as are the
langoustine and fish of the day.
Fixed-price lunches (6400kr) are
decent value given the location,
though dinner is expensive.

Papa's

MAP p.81

Opposite Kvikan museum at Hafnargata
7a, Grindavík ☏ 426 9955, ⊕ papas.is.
Daily noon–10pm.

Grill house serving good cod and
chips (2500kr), though their pizzas
really steal the show: a "supreme"
with everything is 3050kr, but
best is the "TNT", loaded with
pepperoni, black pepper, chillies
and jalapeno sauce (2750kr).

Pylsuvagn

Map p.81

Strandarkirkja, near the campsite.
No phone. Daily 10am–10pm.

This yellow mobile trailer
sells canned drinks and, more
importantly, *pylsur*: Icelandic
hot dogs served with copious
fried onions and remoulade
sauce (800kr). There's an adjacent
shelter shed with chairs and
tables where you can eat if the
weather's bad.

T-Bær Café

MAP p.81

Between the campsite and church,
Strandarkirkja ☏ 483 3150. Mon–Wed &
Fri–Sun 10am–10pm, Thurs 2–10pm.

A long, low wooden building in
the middle of nowhere which
serves great light meals, coffee
and cakes: try the lamb stew,
cheesecake or pancakes with
rhubarb jam (each around
1700kr). Often surprisingly busy
given the location. Not much
English spoken.

Thai Keflavík

MAP p.81

Hafnargata 39, Keflavík ☏ 421 8666,
⊕ thaikeflavik.is. Mon–Fri 11.30am–
10pm, Sat & Sun 4–10pm.

This place, with a plain white
interior and wooden tables, is
popular for its good-value spicy
soups, noodles, red curries and
deep fried fish (nothing over
2700kr). The best deal, though, is
probably their lunchtime buffet
at 1890kr.

The Golden Circle

Spreading eastwards from Reykjavík, the route known as the Golden Circle ties together some of Iceland's most iconic landscapes and historic sights. The centrepiece is Þingvellir, a monumental rift valley where Iceland's original parliament met in Viking times, while the nearby cathedral at Skálholt once served as one of the country's two greatest religious pivots (along with Hólar in northern Iceland). Elsewhere, a web of roads weaves through the lush summertime landscape of meadows framed by distant snowcapped peaks, where you could spend a mellow half-day comparing the relative attractions of outdoor hot pools at Fontana Spa (luxurious) and the so-called "Secret Lagoon" (minimalist). Routes ultimately converge right on the edge of Iceland's barren wilds at Geysir, the original geyser after which all others are named, and the mighty waterfall of Gullfoss.

Þingvellir National Park

MAP p.88, POCKET MAP U1
30km northeast of Reykjavík on Route 36
Ⓦ thingvellir.is/english.aspx. Free.

Þingvellir – the "Assembly Plains" – fill a 4km-wide, 40m-deep rift valley that marks where the North American and Eurasian continental plates are tearing apart at the rate of 1.5cm every year. It was in this dramatic landscape that Iceland's entire population first gathered in the tenth century to hold an annual assembly, thereby establishing a system of government which survived, in one form or another, for nearly a thousand years (see box opposite).

Orientate yourself at the **viewpoint** next to the Visitor Centre on Route 36. South lies Iceland's largest lake, **Þingvallavatn**, from where the rift valley runs northeast for 16km, covered in a tangle of dwarf birch thickets and flanked by basalt columns, to Skjaldbreiður's distant, flattened cone – at 1060m, one of the highest peaks in view.

From the viewpoint, a footpath descends into the 2km-long **Almannagjá canyon** past Lögberg, the rock from where Iceland's laws were publicly recited in Viking times. Look out too for traces of *buðs*, roofed camps built as accommodation during assemblies. The path continues to where the narrow **Öxará** – the Axe River – splashes down into the rift over the western escarpment; the rocks midstream are barely worn, supporting the story that the river was diverted during the tenth century to provide drinking water for the thirty thousand or so people who converged on Þingvellir each year. Under medieval Danish law, the site became an execution ground for witches and adulterers.

East over the river, Þingvellir's plain white **church** sits on a small rise, the only substantial building in the valley. The original structure was built in 1080 with support from the Norwegian king, though the present building dates from 1859. Two tombs out the back belong to the poets

The Alþing

From 960, Iceland's 36 regional chieftains convened the **Alþing**, or General Assembly, at Þingvellir for two weeks every summer. Almost the entire Icelandic population attended the event: tented camps were set up, people traded, gossiped, settled disputes at the four regional courts and listened to the **Lawspeaker** reciting the country's legal code. The highest penalty was being declared an "out-law" – banishment from Iceland for three years – yet, although the courts carried great authority, they had no concrete powers to enforce their decisions beyond making them public knowledge. If litigants felt themselves strong enough to ignore the courts they could do so, though at the risk that others would seek satisfaction privately. *Njál's Saga* (see box, p.96) contains a graphic account of such a battle between two feuding clans, which broke out at the Alþing itself in 1011 AD.

It was the Alþing's lack of real power that allowed Norway and then Denmark to take control of the country during the Middle Ages; by the late thirteenth century the lawspeaker's position was abolished and the courts stripped of all legislative authority. Though Iceland's Alþing survives to this day, restored with full powers after Independence from Denmark in 1944, the **last assembly** at Þingvellir was in 1798, after which the parliament relocated to Reykjavík.

Einar Benediktsson and Jónas Hallgrímsson, both major forces in Iceland's nineteenth-century drive for political independence from Denmark; it's fitting that they were buried in a location so strongly tied to the national identity. While you're here, don't overlook **Flosagjá** and **Peningagjá**, deep volcanic fissures nearby, flooded by clear blue spring water.

Þingvellir National Park

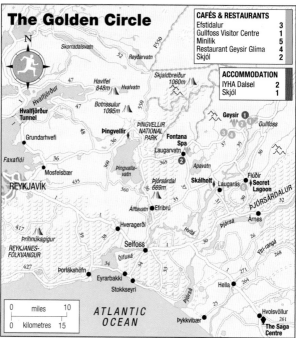

The Golden Circle

CAFÉS & RESTAURANTS	
Efstidalur	3
Gullfoss Visitor Centre	1
Minilik	5
Restaurant Geysir Glíma	4
Skjól	2

ACCOMMODATION	
IYHA Dalsel	2
Skjól	1

Fontana Spa

MAP ABOVE, POCKET MAP V2
Hverabraut 1, Laugarvatn, 75km east of
Reykjavík; turn off Route 37 at the N1
roadhouse and follow the signs Ⓦ fontana
.is. Daily: early June to late Aug 10am–
11pm; rest of year 11am–10pm. 4200kr.

This small open-air spa overlooks
the lakeshore at the tiny resort town
of **Laugarvatn** – which, in typical
Icelandic style, isn't much more
than a few houses. **Fontana** itself
sits literally on top of a cauldron
of bubbling hot springs, which
splutter and hiss noisily below the
sauna huts, pouring out erratic
clouds of steam. There are also a
couple of more sedate tiled thermal
pools; they're very shallow, though
– better for sitting in with a beer
ordered from the bar (there's also
a café that serves light meals) than
for swimming. Visiting after dark
in winter is quite an experience,
especially when the northern lights
are putting on a show.

Skálholt

MAP ABOVE, POCKET MAP U2
Off Route 35 on Route 31, 85km east
of Reykjavík, Ⓦ skalholt.is. Daily
10am–5pm. Free.

The lush farming region above
the middle Hvítá – one of
Iceland's longest rivers – is

Fontana Spa

known as the "Bishop's Tongue". That might be because this is church land, overlooked from the top of a knoll by the historic **Skálholt cathedral**, which was founded as early as 1056 AD (Christianity had only been introduced in 1000 AD). The site went on to become a bustling centre of learning with a population in excess of two hundred people, making it the country's largest medieval settlement. The original wooden cathedral was eventually destroyed by an earthquake in the late eighteenth century, and the current cathedral – an unfussy black-and-white building – was only built and reconsecrated in 1963.

The **interior** is fairly sober too, with abstract stained-glass windows and a tapestry-like mosaic of Christ behind the altar providing the only colour. During the summer, the stone sarcophagus belonging to Bishop Páll Jónsson, a charismatic thirteenth-century churchman, is also on view to the public.

Outside, recent archeological excavations have exposed the foundations of the former bishop's residence. There's also a monument to Iceland's last Catholic bishop, Jón Arason, who was executed here during the religious wars of the sixteenth century.

Skálholt

Secret Lagoon

MAP OPPOSITE, POCKET MAP V2
Off Route 30, at Hverahólmi, Flúðir, 100km east of Reykjavík; head north out of town and turn east immediately over the bridge ☏ 555 3351, ⓦ gamlalaugin.is. Daily: May–Sept 10am–10pm; Oct–April 11am–8pm. 2800kr.

In contrast to the higher-profile Blue Lagoon and Fontana Spa, the "**Secret Lagoon**" is a decidedly low-tech affair – basically a large outdoor pond full of gently steaming water. Purpose-built for recreation in the 1890s, it fell into disrepair after more modern swimming pools sprung up in neighbouring towns, and has only recently been renovated and reopened for general use.

Touring the Golden Circle

Renting a car (see p.124) is the least expensive way for more than one person to cover the Golden Circle, even after factoring in fuel costs. Otherwise, the cheapest deal is on the daily Þingvellir–Laugarvatn–Geysir–Gullfoss **bus** run by Reykjavík Excursions (9750kr return; ⓦ re.is), which stops long enough at each place to have a brief look around. For a dedicated, nine-hour **Golden Circle Tour**, there's Reykjavík Excursions again (9900kr), Gray Line (ⓦ grayline.is; 9500kr) and Sterna (ⓦ sternatravel.com; 11,900kr), not to mention a host of smaller operators. It's best to book a day in advance in summer; all can collect from Reykjavík accommodation, and a guide provides commentary in English en route.

Geysir

MAP p.88, POCKET MAP V1
Right beside Route 35, 100km east
of Reykjavík. Open access. Free.

The **Geysir** thermal area occupies
the edge of a grassy plain below
Bjaranarfell's 720m-high slopes,
with steam from the dozen or
so geysers here visible long
before you arrive. The largest
vent, **Geysir** itself, has been
pretty much inactive for the last
few decades. Instead, join the
crowds surrounding **Strokkur**,
"the Churn", which reliably fires
its load 30m skywards every few
minutes. Nobody is sure exactly
what causes the eruptions, but
watch closely and you'll see a
dome of cooler water form on
top of Strokkur's pool just before
an eruption, which some experts
believe acts as a "lid", allowing
the pressure below to build up to
bursting point. Take time to look
at some of the smaller, less active
vents, especially **Blesi**'s twin
pools – one clear and colourless,
the other opaque blue. There are
no protective barriers at Geysir,
in spite of the boiling hot pools;
keep children supervised and
under no circumstances put any
part of your body in the springs.

Strokkur

Gullfoss

MAP p.88, POCKET MAP V1
Route 35, about 107km east of Reykjavík.
Open access. Free.

Saved for the nation from being
flooded by a hydro dam back in
the 1920s, **Gullfoss** – the Golden
Falls – forms a spectacular,
thundering twin cataract across
the Hvítá River: entering the
mouth of a basalt gorge, the
river drops 10m and then turns
sharply, falling a further 20m
into a sunless chasm from which
spray fountains upwards in huge,
soggy clouds, catching rainbows
and giving the falls their name.
Adding to the spectacle is the
location: look back the way
you've come and all is green,
but turn north and vistas take
in a stark gravel plain spreading
towards the distant mountain
ridges and ice caps of Iceland's
barren Interior (see p.104). In
winter, the canyon is covered
in curtains of ice, and the falls,
brought nearly to a standstill by
the freeze, are eerily silent. The
best viewing place is from the top
of the gorge; you can also walk
right up to the canyon's edge
above the waterfall, but take care
on the wet rocks. Note that there
are no substantial safety barriers
at the site.

Gullfoss

Cafés and restaurants

Efstidalur

MAP p.88
Route 37, about 15km east from Laugarvatn and Fontana Spa towards Geysir ⏰ 486 1186, 🌐 efstidalur.is. Mon–Thurs & Sun 11.30am–8pm, Fri & Sat 11.30–9pm.

Smart hotel restaurant surrounded by beautiful farmland, serving the best food in the region, much of it locally sourced. Try smoked trout or soup (1550–2100kr), or a home-reared steak (5100kr).

Gullfoss Visitor Centre

MAP p.88
Gullfoss, by the car park and lookout 🌐 gullfoss.is/cafe. Daily 9am–9.30pm.

Timber-framed building with glass feature windows offering superlative mountain views. Try their lamb stew (2100kr); much else is ordinary and overpriced.

Minilik

MAP p.88
Hrunamannavegur (Route 30), Flúðir ⏰ 846 9798, 🌐 minilik.is. Opening hours variable, so call ahead to check.

Iceland's sole Ethiopian restaurant is loudly striped in green, yellow and red. Dishes are tangy, sour and spicy and served with traditional

Efstidalur

njeera, (fermented dough pancakes) – try them with *awaze tibs* (a fried lamb dish). Plenty of vegetarian options, and excellent coffee. Bank on around 3000kr a head.

Restaurant Geysir Glíma

MAP p.88
At the Visitor Centre, Geysir 🌐 geysirglima .is. Daily 10am–5pm.

Despite the chic, Nordic-minimalist decor (pine ceiling, slate floor and basalt-block walls), and its obvious tourist trap potential, prices are pretty reasonable here: you can get quiche and salad for 1790kr or a pizza from 1550kr, with even better deals in the separate canteen around the corner. This was the site of Iceland's first wrestling school, hence the unusual photo display.

Skjól

MAP p.88
Route 35, halfway between Geysir and Gullfoss ⏰ 899 4541. Daily from late morning until midnight.

This dark timber, lodge-style bar, out in a lonely field between two of Iceland's most touristed attractions (the owner clearly knew what they was doing when they picked this location), is good for a convivial after-tour drink, conversation and bar snack, though they also do tasty pizza and grills for under 2500kr.

Restaurant Geysir Glíma

The south coast and Heimaey

Heading east from Reykjavík, Highway 1 (the Ringroad) runs parallel to the coast for 185km through a well-watered region of rolling green pasture – home to Iceland's major horse stud farms – and down to the country's southernmost point near the pleasant seaside village of Vík. The final third of the journey passes within sight of the Eyjafjallajökull and Mýrdalsjökull ice caps; Eyjafjallajökull's 1666m apex is southwestern Iceland's highest point, and site of the volcanic eruption in 2010 which grounded aircraft across Europe. Along the way are hothouses at Hveragerði, some key saga landscapes, stunning waterfalls at Seljalandsfoss and Skógar, one of the country's best hiking trails, plus some bizarre black-sand beaches. Offshore, a ferry can whisk you over to impressive cliffs, volcanoes and puffin colonies at Heimaey, largest of the Westman Islands.

Hveragerði

MAP p.94, POCKET MAP U2
Ringroad, 40km southeast of Reykjavík.
Tourist office inside the shopping centre at the entrance to town: Mon–Fri 9am–6pm, Sat 9am–4pm, Sun 9am–2pm ☏ 483 4601, ⓦ south.is. Geothermal Park at Hveramörk

Hveragerði

13. Mon–Fri 9am–5pm, Sat & Sun 9am–1pm. 250kr, mud bath 750kr.

Sitting astride a patently active geothermal area, **Hveragerði** comprises a compact grid of homes just north of the Ringroad, all overlooked by a crumpled mass of steaming hills. This was the first place in Iceland to harness underground heat for agriculture back in the 1920s, and almost half the buildings in town are **hothouses**, growing a year-round supply of fresh vegetables and exotic, colourful garden plants. Other attractions include a **crevasse** which opened up during an earthquake in 2008 and today runs right through the tourist office, and a **Geothermal Park** by the church, which sports steaming vents, bubbling mud pools and even a miniature geyser. Ask at the tourist office about half-day **hiking trails** into the hills behind town, where there are more hissing steam vents and a shallow thermal stream in which you can enjoy a warm soak.

Selfoss

MAP p.94, POCKET MAP U2
Ringroad, 57km southeast of Reykjavík; Kerið crater is 15km north on Route 35.

The main landmark at **Selfoss**, a large service town on the fast-flowing Ölfusá, is its substantial **suspension bridge** (Ölfusárbrú), which first opened in 1891 and immediately drew business away from the small river ferry which used to operate downstream. Homes and shops set up around the new crossing, and gradually Iceland's first inland town took shape. The original bridge – whose construction caused a major strike, after labourers were only given fresh salmon to eat – collapsed in 1944, though, when two milk trucks tried to cross it at the same time. It was rebuilt in under 6 months, reopening in 1945. Aside from this, the sole sight nearby is little **Kerið** crater, a 70m-deep, flooded volcanic depression formed from deep red scoria gravel. Selfoss is also something of a gateway: the Ringroad continues eastwards over the well-watered plains of the lower Þjórsá and Rangá river systems, while north are routes to the Golden Circle and Interior.

Kerið

Stokkseyri and Eyrarbakki

MAP p.94, POCKET MAP U3
Route 34, 15km south of Selfoss. Ghost Centre at Hafnargata 9, Stokkseyri Ⓦ **icelandicwonders.is. 2000kr.**

Insignificant today, these two pretty seaside villages have a rich historical heritage – and excellent **restaurants** (see p.101). The former fishing hamlet of **Stokkseyri** was once an important port, though when you stand on the stone storm wall and gaze out across the seaweed-strewn rocks and reefs, it's hard to imagine fishermen launching their heavy rowing boats from such an inhospitable shore. The old fish-processing factory incorporates a **Ghost Centre**, a slightly tacky take on Icelandic folklore.

About 4km west, larger **Eyrarbakki** houses a prison and an attractive core of old wooden homes, but is principally famous for being where Bjarni Herjólfsson set sail in 985 AD, on a voyage which took him within sight of North America (albeit accidentally). He later told Leifur Eiríksson about his discovery, and so it was Leifur who became the first known European to make landfall in the Americas – or "Vinland" as he called it, after the vines that grew there.

Stokkseyri

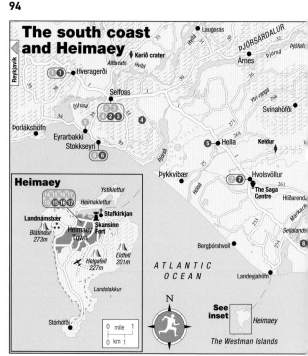

Keldur

MAP ABOVE, POCKET MAP V3
Off the Ringroad 95km southeast of Reykjavík, then 20km north on Route 264, the final few kilometres on a good gravel road. June–Aug daily 10am–6pm. 1200kr.

Though a little off the beaten track, saga associations make the detour to **Keldur** a rewarding trip. This pretty farm sits amid fields on the edge of an overgrown lava flow, with the cloud-smudged **Hekla volcano** (see p.106) as a backdrop. Most of its buildings are recent, but the estate dates to Viking times and parts of a traditional turf-roofed block here might well be over eight hundred years old: the structural beams are dated to the seventeenth century, but wall panels are decorated with simple line engravings, typical of the Viking period. Of similar vintage is the rough-hewn **tunnel** under the house (sometimes open to the public), which was built as an escape route in case of siege. It's believed that **Snorri Sturluson**, Iceland's great medieval man of letters, was raised at Keldur.

The Saga Centre

MAP ABOVE, POCKET MAP V3
100km southeast of Reykjavík along the Ringroad at Hlíðarvegur 14, Hvolsvöllur ☏ 487 8781 , ⊕ njala.is. May 15–Sept 15 daily 9am–6pm; Sept 15–May 15 Sat & Sun 10am–5pm. 900kr.

Hvolsvöllur's absorbing **Saga Centre** needs a good hour of your time. Most of the museum explores the Viking period through detailed information boards, photos of important sites, models, dioramas, replicas of clothes and weapons, and maps of the routes that these great naval navigators and explorers took on their wanderings. Ask too about progress on a modern project to create a 90m-long, Bayeux-like **tapestry** of *Njál's Saga* (see box,

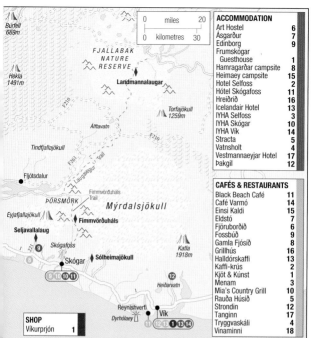

p.96), featuring all the major episodes from the tale.

The Lava Centre

MAP ABOVE, POCKET MAP V3
Austurvegur 14, Hvolsvöllur, Ringroad 100km southeast of Reykjavík ☎ 415 5200, ⊕ lavacentre.is. Daily 9am–7pm. 3200kr; cinema only 1200kr; exhibition only 2400kr.

The **Lava Centre**, housed in a long, low modernist building by the Ringroad, offers a fun and informative introduction to Iceland's geology and vulcanology. Interactive exhibits give a rundown of country's historic eruptions, earthquakes and lava spills – and the systems put in place to warn of future events. Southern volcanoes get the fullest treatment: ever-murmuring Hekla, which last erupted in 2000; Katla (worryingly overdue for an eruption); and Eyjafjallajökull, whose 2010 ash cloud buried nearby farms, played havoc with European airlines, and caused amusement in Iceland as foreign newsreaders attempted to pronounce it. Surprisingly for a country with access to some incredible archive footage of these events, the cinema is slightly underwhelming – commentary would help – though the shots of oozing lava are impressive.

The Lava Centre

Njál's Saga

With its hardboiled narrative, a deep streak of dark humour and deadpan descriptions of shocking violence, **Njál's Saga** paints a vivid picture of clan warfare in tenth-century Iceland. The story centres on the life of the far-sighted Njál Þorgeirsson and his great friend, the heroic and generous Gunnar Hámundarson, whose lives are pitched against the evil schemings of Mörð Valgarðsson. Jealous of Gunnar's popularity, Mörð manipulates a succession of disreputable characters into picking fights with him, and Gunnar is eventually branded a troublemaker and exiled from Iceland at the Alþing law courts (see box, p.87). When he refuses to leave, a vengeful posse led by Mörð lays siege to his home, finally killing him after his spiteful wife refuses to help defend the house – inspiring Gunnar's memorable comment, "To each their own way of earning fame".

Meanwhile, encouraged by Mörð, Njál's sons carry out their own vendettas against a rival clan. After peace talks break down, Njál and almost his entire family are driven into their house and burned to death, an event which deeply divides the country. The sole survivor, Kári, chases "the Burners" overseas, where he hunts them down, one at a time. But his anger eventually subsides, and he makes a pilgrimage to seek absolution from the pope before returning to Iceland, where all the players in the saga finally make peace.

Seljalandsfoss

MAP p.94, POCKET MAP V3
120km southeast of Reykjavík at the junction of the Ringroad and Route 249.

East from Hvolsvöllur, just past the turning to Landeyjahöfn and the ferry port for Heimaey (see p.100), Route 249 branches north towards Þórsmörk (see p.108). Almost immediately you reach

Seljalandsfoss, an impressive **waterfall** that drops 60m off the long, undercut hillside into a shallow pool. There are good views from slopes off to one side, and a footpath runs right behind the curtain – expect a good soaking from the spray. It's especially photogenic on summer evenings, when the

Seljalandsfoss

Seljavallalaug

low sun catches the spray and makes the falls glow gold. Walk along the cliff and you'll find several smaller falls too, one of which, **Gljúfrafoss**, is almost hidden inside the cliff-face.

Seljavallalaug

MAP p.94, POCKET MAP W3
Ringroad 140km southeast of Reykjavík,
then north along gravel Route 242 for a
few kilometres to a parking area. Free.

Inland off the Ringroad, and then a fifteen-minute walk along a rubble-filled gorge, **Seljavallalaug** is a fairly shallow, rectangular **swimming pool** fed by a hot spring. It was just about buried by ash in the 2010 Eyjafjallajökull eruption – though you can't see the ice cap itself from here, you're right under the edge of the Eyjafjallajökull plateau – but the pool is now clean again, and having an outdoor soak amid the wild scenery is a memorable and quintessentially Icelandic experience.

Fimmvörðuháls hike

The 25km-long trail from **Skógar** (see p.98) to **Þórsmörk** (see p.108), via the Fimmvörðuháls pass between the Eyjafjallajökull and Mýrdalsjökull ice caps, is one of Iceland's best – and most demanding – day hikes. It's usually accessible without equipment from mid-June to September, though you always need to come prepared for rain and snow, poor visibility and cold. The track is erratically pegged, so carry a compass and a suitable map.

From the top of Skógarfoss the trail follows the river uphill past many small **waterfalls**. Some 8km along there's a footbridge and the landscape changes to a dark, rocky plain, gradually climbing to snowfields. Along the way you pass **two hiking huts** (you need to book beds via Ⓦ utivist.is) and a pale blue tarn at **Fimmvörðuháls** (1043m), the flat pass in between the two glaciers. You end up at the top of a steep, 100m snowfield with dramatic views down into Þórsmörk; the quickest way down is to cautiously slide it on your backside. At the bottom is a short but scary traverse across a narrow ledge to the flat, muddy plateau of **Morinsheiði**, from where a relatively straightforward descent lands you at Þórsmörk. Allow at least eight hours for the journey, even in good weather.

THE SOUTH COAST AND HEIMAEY

Skógar

MAP p.94, POCKET MAP W4
Ringroad, 155km southeast of Reykjavík.
Folk Museum ⓦ skogasafn.is. Daily: June–
Aug 9am–6pm; Sept–May 10am–5pm.
2000kr.

There's very little to the hamlet of **Skógar** – not even a proper shop or fuel pump – and there'd be no reason to stop if it weren't for a stunning waterfall, plus an unusually interesting museum. Invisible from the road, the waterfall – **Skógarfoss** – is a 62m-high monster: stand in front of it (if the outward blast of air doesn't knock you over) and the world disappears amid roaring waters and spray. There's a metal staircase to the top and the start of the muddy moorland trail up over the mountains towards Þórsmörk (see p.108), with long views seawards out to Heimaey.

Across the hamlet, Skógar's **Folk Museum** sketches out the region's history through an eclectic collection which takes in everything from nineteenth-century wooden fishing boats and turf farmhouses to a copy of the Bible dating from 1584, a Viking cloak pin, and a brass ring from a treasure chest which some stingy farmer – who didn't want his children to inherit his wealth – had thrown into the pool at Skógarfoss.

Sólheimajökull

MAP p.94, POCKET MAP W3
153km southeast along the Ringroad from
Reykjavík, then 5km north along the gravel
Route 221.

Immediately over the shallow, glacier-fed Jökulsá Fulilækur, turn north off the Ringroad and follow the track to a parking area. From here it's a fifteen-minute walk to the front of **Sólheimajökull**, a narrow but substantial **glacier** descending off the Mýrdalsjökull ice cap. As they move under their own colossal weight, Iceland's glaciers grind the rocks below into black gravel and sand which makes the ice tongues look "dirty", but Sólheimajökull is certainly impressive, deeply streaked in crevasses. Don't approach too close, as the glacier front is unstable.

Skógarfoss

View from Dyrhólaey

Dyrhólaey

MAP p.94, POCKET MAP W4
165km southeast along the Ringroad from
Reykjavík, then 6km south on Route 218.
Dyrhólaey is Iceland's
southernmost point, a dramatic
set of basalt cliffs jutting out to
sea over a long expanse of black
sand. There's a lighthouse, and the
cliffs are pierced by a huge arch
– not visible from here, though
Black Beach Café (see p.101) at
Reynishverfi makes a fine vantage
point – that is large enough for a
yacht to pass beneath. Dyrhólaey's
grassy tops are also riddled
with puffin burrows, occupied
by breeding birds throughout
the summer.

Reynishverfi

MAP p.94, POCKET MAP W4
175km southeast of the Ringroad from
Reykjavík, then 6km south on Route 215.
East of Dyrhólaey the view is
blocked by Reynisfjall, a ridge
of hills running to the sea. At its
southwestern tip lies **Reynishverfi**,
an attractive shingle beach with
treacherous waves (don't get too
close) and a steep cliff faced in
twisted basalt columns. Down the
beach is a large cave, while the
offshore stacks are the Troll Rocks,
which are better viewed from Vík.

Vík

MAP p.94, POCKET MAP X4
Ringroad, 185km southeast of Reykjavík.
A pretty coastal village caught
between Reynisfjall's steep, sodden
slopes and a deadening expanse
of volcanic desert to the east, **Vík**
started life as a trading station
during the nineteenth century and
has since expanded to fill a few
streets. The only sight in town is
Brydebúð, the original wooden
general store around which Vík
coalesced, which now serves as an
information centre, local history
museum, and a restaurant. The
road runs 500m past Brydebúð
and down to a parking bay
above the sea, beyond which lies
Reynisfjall's southernmost cliffs,
packed with nesting seabirds,
three tall spires offshore known
as Reynisdrangar – the **Troll
Rocks** – and a long, **black-sand
beach** stretching eastwards to the
horizon.

Getting to Heimaey

The Herjólfur car and passenger **ferry** to Heimaey (☎ 482 2800, Ⓦ herjolfur.is) departs several times a day from **Landeyjahöfn**, 15km south off the Ringroad at Seljalandsfoss (see p.96) via Route 254. Pedestrians 1380kr each way; cars 2780kr plus 1380kr/person. For **flights from Reykjavík** contact Eagle Air (☎ 562 2640, Ⓦ eagleair.is). The fare is 19,000kr each way, with online discounts available.

Heimaey

MAP p.94, POCKET MAP V4
Natural History Museum, Heiðarvegur 12 Ⓦ saeheimar.is. May–Sept daily 10am–5pm; Oct–April Sat 1–4pm. 1200kr. Eldheimar museum, Helgafellsbraut ☎ 488 2000, Ⓦ eldheimar.is. Daily 11am–6pm. 2300kr including audioguide.

The volcanic **Westman Islands**, 10km off Iceland's southwest coast, all formed over the last few thousand years – though the youngest, Surtsey, popped out of the waves as recently as the 1960s.

The only inhabited island in the group, **Heimaey**, is also the largest at 6km long, and the ferry (see box above) docks alongside fishing boats right in the middle of Heimaey town. Aim first for the **Natural History Museum**, where the highlight is a tame, orphaned puffin which you can handle. Around the harbour, Skansinn is a reconstructed thirteenth-century stone fort, while **Stafkirkjan** is a traditional wooden church, built in the Viking style in 2000. Inland, paths lead through the rough mass of the Kirkjubærhraun lavafield and up to the summit of Eldfell volcano, whose 1973 eruption nearly destroyed the town. For more on this event, visit the superb **Eldheimar museum**, built around the excavated remains of a house which was completely buried under ash. To see puffins in the wild you'll need to hike 6km south to Stórhöfði headland, whose grassy slopes are riddled through summer with their burrows.

Stafkirkjan, Heimaey

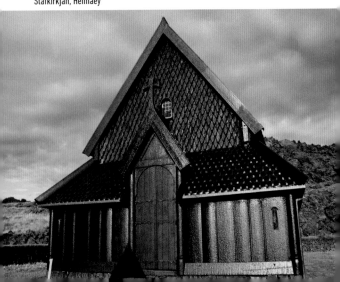

Shop

Víkurprjón

MAP p.94
Next to the N1 fuel station on the Ringroad,
Vík Ⓦ icewear.is. Daily 7.30am–10.30pm.

This factory outlet has made a
name for itself in the quality
of its woollens – everything from
traditional heavy-duty Icelandic
jumpers to hats, gloves and
blankets. The ground floor has all
the tourist tat; head upstairs for
outdoor wear and lower prices.

Cafés and restaurants

Black Beach Café

MAP p.94
Reynishverfi ☏ 571 2718, Ⓦ blackbeach.is.
Daily 11am–10pm; à la carte 6–9pm.

A modern glass-fronted affair,
built of black basalt blocks and
perfectly camouflaged against the
cliffs, this makes a perfect spot
to withdraw from bad weather
and enjoy a warming bowl of
lamb soup (1850kr), fish and
chips (2590kr) or just a cake and
coffee (990kr). Don't miss the
superb views down the coast to
Dyrhólaey's arch (see p.99).

Café Varmó

MAP p.94
At the corner of Herjolfsgata and
Strandvegur, Heimaey ☏ 481 1674.
Mon–Fri 10am–6pm.

The plain, dated decor won't win
any prizes, but prices are fair and
if you like heavy-duty home-made
cakes, or hearty lamb and barley
soup that you could stand a spoon
up in, you're in the right place.

Einsi Kaldi

MAP p.94
At the Vestmannaeyjar Hotel,
Vestmannabraut 28, Heimaey ☏ 481 2900,
Ⓦ einsikaldi.is. Daily 11am–2pm & 5–9pm.

Smart and expensive restaurant

inside the town's only real hotel
(see p.119). Safe bets are the
succulent monkfish (3890kr),
lamb fillet with thyme (5690kr)
or the horse tenderloin (5750kr).
If you can't make up your mind
try the three-course set menu, fair
value at 7500kr.

Eldstó

MAP p.94
Austurvegur 2, Hvolsvöllur ☏ 482 1011,
Ⓦ eldsto.is. Restaurant daily 11am–10pm.

Pottery, gallery and café inside a
comfy, old-style timber-and-tin
building. Variable quality, but
on a good day the Greek salad
(2290kr) or tasty baked cod
(3790kr) do the job well. The
cake and coffee is always good
(1100kr).

Fjöruborðið

MAP p.94
Eyrarbraut 3a, Stokkseyri ☏ 483 1550,
Ⓦ fjorubordid.is. Daily noon–9pm.

Lobster restaurants have
flourished in Iceland over the last
few years, and this is one of the
best – not least for the location,
inside a wooden shack up
against the sea wall at no-horse
Stokkseyri village. They sell a
whopping fifteen tons of lobster
a year; a set meal of lobster soup,
300g of langoustine tails and a
dessert costs 9300kr, but you
could always just order the soup
(3350kr) or 250g of tails (5300kr).

Fossbúð

MAP p.94
On the road to the falls, Skógar
☏ 487 8843. Daily 7am–9pm.

Run by the nearby *Hótel Skógar*,
this restaurant serves basic,
filling, plain food – sandwiches,
burgers, soup, buns and chips
– at very reasonable prices.
The lunchtime special of pork
schnitzel, soup and coffee costs
3500kr, and will be very welcome
if you've just hiked in from
Þórsmörk.

Kjöt & Kúnst

Gamla Fjósíð

MAP p.94
Ringroad, about 10km west of Skógar ⓣ 487 7788, ⓦ gamlafjosid.is. Daily 11am–9pm.

Housed in a low-ceilinged former cowshed, this comfortable café-restaurant dishes up a range of tasty dishes – everything from burgers (2070kr) to Westman Islands lobster (6920kr) or catch of the day (3990kr). It's perhaps best known, though, for its "Volcano soup", a beef stew laden with chillies (2390kr).

Grillhús

MAP p.94
Vestmannabraut, across from the Vestmannaeyjar, Heimaey ⓣ 482 1000. Mon–Fri & Sun 11am–10pm, Sat 11am–11.30pm.

No surprises what they serve at this low-slung timber-clad diner: T-bone steak (4990kr), lobster burgers (2690kr), fish and chips (2190kr) and pizza. The delicious scent of barbecued meat wafts around the street outside while they're serving.

Halldórskaffi

MAP p.94
Inside Brydebúð, Vík ⓣ 487 1202. Daily 11am–8pm.

About half of this old timber building is a dining room, but it still can't cope with the crowds who come for their superb pizzas: a 12" seafood special with shrimps, mussels and tuna costs 3200kr. They don't take bookings, so turn up prepared to wait – luckily, it's worth it.

Kaffi-krús

MAP p.94
Austurvegur, Selfoss ⓣ 482 1266 , ⓦ kaffikrus.is. Daily 10am–10pm.

One of the longest-running cafés outside the capital, this cosy, low-ceilinged place is best for fine coffee, cakes and light meals (eaten on the terrace in good weather), though they also do some pricey mains – burgers, salmon or grills – at upwards of 2500kr.

Kjöt & Kúnst

MAP p.94
Breiðamörk 21, Hveragerði ⓣ 483 5010, ⓦ kjotogkunst.is. Mon–Sat noon–8.30pm.

Pouring out clouds of steam on cold days, it's hard to miss the thermal ovens outside this place, which they put to good use in preparing fish and meat dishes (5500kr) – not to mention their famous *hverabrauð* (steam-baked rye bread). Not bad either for salads, grills, soup and meatballs (around 2500kr), or just a hot cup of coffee.

Menam

MAP p.94
Eyravegur 8, Selfoss ☎ 482 4099.
Daily 11.30am–2pm & 5–10pm.

The heat and spices are toned down a bit for local tastes, but *Menam*'s traditional Thai dishes, such as green chicken curry, are packed with flavour and come with a healthy portion of rice. Excellent value, with most mains under 2800kr.

Mia's Country Grill

MAP p.94
Skógar ☎ 696 6542. Summer only, no fixed hours.

You can't miss this bright red polka-dot van serving fresh, crispy fried fish and chips, starting from around 2100kr. One of the best places to eat near Skógarfoss.

Rauða Húsið

MAP p.94
Búðarstíg 4, Eyrarbakki ☎ 483 3330, Ⓦ raudahusid.is. Daily noon–10pm.

Alternative to Stokkseyri's *Fjöruborðið* (see p.101), though there's a wider choice of dishes besides lobster (which is also cheaper here, at 6650kr): fish of the day (4500kr), lamb fillet (5500kr) or a sampler of smoked and cured salmon (2150kr). Don't miss their warm chocolate cake for dessert. Booking essential.

Strondin

MAP p.94
Austurvegur 18, Vík ☎ 487 1230.
Daily 6–10pm.

Facing seawards from behind the N1 roadhouse, *Strondin* has an outdoor terrace and glassed-in dining room for wet days. Though the decor is plain, the menu is varied: dishes cover everything from lamb stew (2300kr) to chicken pasta with basil and tomatoes (2550kr). You could also take a chance on a traditional taster of *hákarl* (fermented shark) with the essential *brennevin* chaser (2450kr).

Tanginn

MAP p.94
Tangagata, Heimaey ☎ 414 4420. Mon–Fri 11am–11pm, Sat & Sun 11am–1am.

Down at the harbour, this dark room with feature windows and heavy pine furniture makes a surprisingly chic setting for feasting on some excellent seafood. The mussels are a good starter (1850kr), best followed by monkfish (3620kr) or cod and chips (3490kr) – though they also serve a not-very-traditional horse fillet. Sea views make it a good place to linger over a beer on a rainy day.

Tryggvaskáli

MAP p.94
Austurvegur 1, on the roundabout by the bridge, Selfoss ☎ 482 1390 Ⓦ tryggvaskali.is. Daily 11.30am–10pm.

Hidden off the roundabout by the bridge, the oldest wooden building in Selfoss makes a smart and quirky setting for enjoying some excellent food – cod and kale (4950kr), lobster salad (4950kr) or slow-cooked salmon and barley (4550kr). The building has served a number of purposes over the years, including a hotel, and the variously sized rooms are still furnished with period fittings.

Vinaminni

MAP p.94
Barustígur, Heimaey ☎ 481 2424.
Daily 10am–10pm.

Not the best place on the island to eat, but long opening hours make this a convenient place to head for a coffee, and the food menu isn't bad: salmon and scrambled egg sandwiches (1250kr), pitta stuffed with various fillings (1900kr) and the inevitable pizzas and burgers (from 1860kr).

The Interior

You'd need to set aside a good week for a comprehensive trip across the heart of Iceland's Interior, a stark landscape of monochrome gravel plains, enormous ice caps and atrocious storms – but you can reach its fringes with an overnight visit. There are Viking remains at Þjórsádalur, a valley ravaged by the twelfth-century eruption of one of Iceland's most active volcanoes, Hekla; an extraordinary hot-spring bathing experience in the wilds at Landmannalaugar; and stunning highland scenery at Þórsmörk, whose horizons are hemmed in by glacier caps. With a little more time, it's also possible to walk between Landmannalaugar and Þórsmörk along one of the country's finest hiking trails – as long as you come equipped for the weather and a few relatively shallow river crossings.

Stöng

MAP OPPOSITE, POCKET MAP W2
115km east from Ryekjavík via Selfoss (see p.93) and Route 32, then 7km north along Route 327, a gravel track that can sometimes be impassable for conventional vehicles.

Iceland's longest river – the Þjórsá – exits the Interior through **Þjórsárdalur**, a once fertile valley which in 1104 was smothered under a thick blanket of volcanic ash during

an eruption of Hekla, only a few kilometres to the east. Up on the valley's eastern side, ongoing excavations since the 1930s have uncovered the well-preserved remains of **Stöng**, the farmstead of Viking chieftain Gaukur Trándilsson. Protected inside a tin-roofed shed, stone foundations and postholes mark the outline of a longhouse, with the central fire pit, various halls, outhouses, animal pens and

Þjóðveldisbærinn

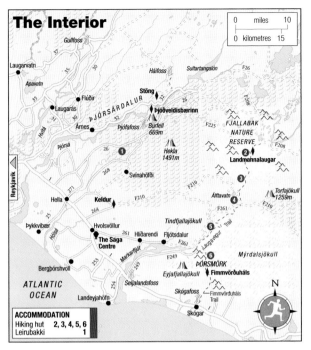

The Interior

private quarters clearly visible. Not on view are an adjoining smithy and church, which were discovered only recently.

Háifoss

MAP ABOVE, POCKET MAP W2
A 20km return hike from the car park at Stöng, or a 12km drive each way along gravel routes 327 and 332, which might be too rough for conventional vehicles.

Northeast up the valley from Stöng, **Háifoss** – Iceland's fourth-highest waterfall – plunges 120m

off the Interior plateau in a single narrow curtain, the deep, narrow canyon below undercut by the force of the water. A second falls upstream is joined to the first by a short but narrow gully.

Þjóðveldisbærinn

MAP ABOVE, POCKET MAP W2
115km east from Ryekjavík via Selfoss (see p.93) and Route 32, then 500m south along a signposted track
ⓦ thjodveldisbaer.is/en. June–Aug daily 10am–6pm. 600kr.

To appreciate how the longhouse at Stöng originally appeared, visit nearby **Þjóðveldisbærinn**, a reconstructed period homestead built from hand-cut timber and roofed in thick slabs of insulating turf. Inside it's surprisingly cosy (though don't forget that livestock were penned here too, at least through the winter), and the bright furnishings suggest a comfortable – if very public – living space.

Seasonal access

Most Interior roads are **four-wheel-drive only**, and even then are open for just a few months each summer, when they're covered by buses and private tours. Check sight accounts for details.

Hekla

Hekla

MAP p.105, POCKET MAP W2
Contact Discover Iceland for guided hikes to the summit; ⓦ discover.is.

With its 1500m-high summit usually hidden by cloud, **Hekla** – one of Iceland's most active volcanoes – is named after an expression meaning "Hooded". The mountain's regular eruptions (including the one that buried Stöng in 1104), disturbing subterranean grumblings and a belief that its sulphurous crater formed the very entrance to hell, left it unclimbed until the eighteenth century; it last stirred in February 2000, when hundreds of sightseers from Reykjavík became trapped on Hekla's foothills by a snowstorm. On clear days, its hunchbacked crest dusted in snow makes an unmistakable landmark, visible from as far away as Selfoss.

Þjófafoss

MAP p.105, POCKET MAP V2
123km east from Reykjavík via the Ringroad and Route 26, then 4km west on a good gravel track.

One of the best views to be had of Hekla is from **Þjófafoss**, a broad, lively waterfall just to the west, which sits below a looming flat-topped hill in a bend of the Þjórsá. You're not only close to Hekla here, but also surrounded by a strangely attractive monochrome landscape of degraded lava and pale yellow pumice pebbles. Despite the apparent desolation and the bumpy gravel road in, this isn't a particularly difficult place to reach, providing an easy taster of the Interior's barren charms.

Landmannalaugar

MAP p.105, POCKET MAP W2
175km east from Reykjavík via the Ringroad, Route 26 and the F225. Route F225 is open June–September and is four-wheel-drive only, involving soft sand and several dangerous river crossings. For summer bus schedules contact Trex (ⓦ trex.is). Jeep day-tours are run by Landmannalaugar Tours (ⓦ landmannalaugartours.com) and Arctic Adventures (ⓦ adventures.is).

Set amid a rugged landscape of shattered obsidian and rhyolite peaks, brightly streaked in orange, grey and green, **Landmannalaugar** is a flat-bottomed gravel valley bordered on one side by a massive fifteenth-century lava flow. Out from underneath the lava emerge two streams, one icy cold and the other scalding hot; there's a perfect wild bathing spot where the waters mix. Known for its summer pasture, Landmannalaugar was once a staging post on cross-Iceland roads, and there are some fine day-hikes in the vicinity – in good weather, don't miss the chance to ascend **Bláhnúkur** (945m), the bald peak to the south, for spectacular views. There's a clearly marked path up the north face to the top, but for a bit of excitement, try a slip-slide descent via the loose scree slopes to the west. For many, however, Landmannalaugar's appeal is in its location at the trailhead for the long-distance Laugavegur hiking route to Þórsmörk and the coast at Skógar.

Laugavegur hike

The superb **Laugavegur hiking trail** stretches 55km between Landmannalaugar and Þórsmörk, divided into stages by huts and campsites which are grouped at regular intervals. From Þórsmörk, you can continue south over the mountains to Skógar via the Fimmvörðuhals pass (see box, p.97).

The first stage (12km) passes a steaming thermal area at Stórihver – a bizarre sight amid the snow – before ending high in the hills at **Hrafntinnusker**, a weather-beaten slope covered in obsidian boulders. From here it's another 12km over a snowy rhyolite plateau and down a steep slope to **Álftavatn**, a small lake set amid vivid green hillocks; the next stage is slightly longer and crosses a gravel desert and a couple of very shallow (but icy cold) rivers to a tiny sheltered valley at **Bótnar-Emstrur**. There are fabulous views of Entujökull, the nearest of Mýrdalsjökull's glaciers, from clifftops around 3km southeast of the hut here. The final 15km leg to **Þórsmörk** (see p.108) is over relatively dull moorland before you ford the Þröngá – the deepest river you have to ford on the trail – and enter the suddenly lush birch and juniper woodland at Þórsmörk's northern boundary, just a short walk from the huts and bus stop.

The trail is open from June until mid-September, when buses run daily from Reykjavík to the end points at Landmannalaugar and Þórsmörk (see ⓦtrex.is for bus schedules). Hikers need to carry their own food and be fully equipped for the weather conditions. For information, contact the Icelandic Touring Association (ⓦfi.is).

Þórsmörk

Þórsmörk

MAP p.105, POCKET MAP W3
155km southeast from Reykjavík via Route 1 and the F249. The F249 is four-wheel-drive only, involving rough gravel and dangerous river crossings, and is only open June–September. For bus schedules contact Trex (W trex.is). Jeep tours run by Midgard Adventure (W midgardadventure.is).

A beautiful highland valley, **Þórsmörk** has hiking trails

Krossá River, Þórsmörk

running in all directions, and thick stands of dwarf willow, birch and wildflowers watered by a web of glacial rivers that flow west off the Mýrdalsjökull ice cap. The valley is split into three areas, each with its own hiking hut accommodation; isolated on the far western side is Húsadalur (W volcanohuts.com), Þórsmörk's main bus terminus but still a thirty-minute hike from the main valley. This is split in two by the 7km-long Krossá River, a braided glacial flow which originates in the ice caps that hem everything in; to the north of the river is Þórsmörk proper, with a base of sorts at Skagfjörðsskáli hut (W fi. is), while to the south is Goðaland and Básar hut (W utivist.is). Be sure to cross the Krossá via the bridge; the river is dangerously cold and fast, and people have drowned trying to wade over. The best views on the river's north side are from the top of knuckle-like Valahnúkur, a brief hike up on a well-marked path; south of the Krossá lies a more challenging climb in the shape of 805m-hig Útigönguhöfði – the final section is incredibly steep, with chains to help you.

Þórsmörk hikes

Þórsmörk is covered in a network of excellent **hiking trails**, though these are not well marked on the ground and even "easy" routes tend to involve steep gradients, loose scree and occasionally high, narrow traverses. Rangers at the accommodation huts can provide useful maps, weather forecasts and general advice, though – hardened as they are to local conditions – they often underestimate potential difficulties.

The main walk from the **Skagfjörðsskáli** hut starts at the next bay east at Slyppugil, a wooded gully which you follow uphill to the jagged east–west ridge of Tindfjöll. The trail weaves along Tindfjöll's gravelly, landslip-prone north face to the solitary spire of Tröllakirkja, before emerging onto open heathland at Tindfjöll's eastern end: the double-tipped cone 2km northeast is Rjúpnafell, which you can climb via a steep, zigzagging path up to its 824m summit – give yourself at least five hours for the return hike from the hut.

The best excursion from the **Básar** hut is to follow the popular trail south towards Skógar (see p.98) as far as the flat, muddy Morinsheiði Plateau. From here you turn west and descend to a low saddle below 805m-high Útigönguhöfði, then take a hideously steep path straight up it to the rounded peak. Views from the top are breathtaking, and there's a chain to help your descent off the far side. A low, 5km-long ridge continues west to the heights directly above Básar, with an easy descent along a path to your starting point. Again, allow five hours for the hike.

Hiking in Þórsmörk

ACCOMMODATION

Icelandair Reykjavík Marina

Accommodation

Although Reykjavík's accommodation options continue to mushroom as the tourist influx increases, pressure on beds in the summer months is always great and it's a good idea to book in advance, especially in June, July and August. Hotels do not come cheap in Reykjavík, usually hovering around 25,000–35,000kr for an average double room in high season. The quality is, however, generally high, though rooms can be block-like and characterless – sometimes it's the view or the location that makes it. Online discounts and opting for a shared bathroom (where available) can reduce prices significantly. Guesthouses cost around 15,000–20,000kr; often family run, they tend to have more character than hotels, with rooms ranging from the barely furnished to the very comfortable, and facilities are usually shared. Prices overall tend to rise by around a third during the high season (May to September); those given here are for the cheapest double room during the summer months.

At hostels, you'll find that meals are sometimes offered, though most have kitchens for self-catering. Campsites vary in size but will always have washing facilities, and sometimes a kitchen, too. Self-catering is worth considering since it will save a lot of money on eating out – one of the main expenses in Iceland.

Lækjartorg, Austurstræti and Austurvöllur

BORG MAP p.28, POCKET MAP D4. Pósthússtræti 11 ☎ 551 1440, ⓦ hotelborg.is. The city's very first hotel, opened in the 1930s and the unofficial home of visiting heads of state ever since. A showcase of sophistication and four-star elegance, each room is individually decorated in Art Deco style with period furniture – and prices to match. It's hard to beat the location, too, right in the heart of the Austurvöllur area, with Austurstræti and Hafnarstræti right on the doorstep. **45,000kr**

PLAZA MAP p.28, POCKET MAP C3. Aðalstræti 4 ☎ 595 8550, ⓦ centerhotels.com. The style in this tastefully renovated old building, a stone's throw from Austurstræti, is Nordic minimalism meets old-fashioned charm, with heavy wooden floors, plain white walls and immaculately tiled bathrooms complementing the high-beamed ceilings. The rooms at the front of the hotel look out over Ingólfstorg which can be noisy so it may be wise to seek out a room further back. **30,200kr**

RADISSON BLU 1919 MAP p.28, POCKET MAP D3. Pósthússtræti 2 ☎ 599 1000, ⓦ radissonblu.com/1919hotel-reykjavik. Housed in the elegant former headquarters of the Eimskip shipping line, this Art Deco hotel combines old-fashioned charm with modern chic. Book one month in advance to secure the rate we have given. The penthouse suites (77,400kr) with elevated sleeping sections and separate dining area are the best Reykjavík has to offer and

Booking ahead

In order to get the lowest room rate book well in advance via the hotel's own website or try one of the many online booking sites. If you do arrive at the last minute without a reservation, the city tourist office may be able to help at their office on Aðalstræti (see p.129). Alternatively, think about staying in Hafnarfjörður (see p.76), where pressure on beds is less intense.

would make an ideal treat for a special occasion. 39,000kr

REYKJAVÍK CENTRUM MAP p.28, POCKET MAP C4. Aðalstræti 16 📞 514 6000, 🌐 hotelcentrum.is. Built in traditional early-1900s style, this hotel offers a curious yet pleasing mix of stylish and homely, featuring old-fashioned wallpapers and fittings. Perfectly located on Aðalstræti, it's near the action of Laugavegur as well as being ideally situated for a gentle evening stroll around Tjörnin, which is right on the doorstep. Breakfast is an extra 2700kr. 37,000kr

The harbour

CAPTAIN REYKJAVÍK MAP p.41, POCKET MAP B3. Ránargata 11 📞 695 4866, 🌐 captainreykjavik.is. In a quiet location only a few minutes' walk from both the harbour and the city centre, this friendly guesthouse offers plain but clean and bright rooms. The triples are a bit silly, though, with the third bed basically on top of the cupboard. Rooms share facilities, but the price for a double easily undercuts the nearby *Downtown Hostel*. Breakfast around 550kr extra. 16,400kr

ICELANDAIR REYKJAVÍK MARINA MAP p.41, POCKET MAP B1. Mýrargata 2 📞 444 4000, 🌐 icelandairhotels.com. Bold, brash and refreshingly quirky, this harbourside hotel not only enjoys terrific views of the trawlers in dry dock right outside, but its rooms also have a maritime feel with a twist of chic. If you're on a stopover deal with Icelandair (see box, p.122), or are simply booking accommodation via the airline and are able to choose between this hotel and the *Icelandair Reykjavík Natura* (see p.116), make this one your preference. 40,000kr

REYKJAVÍK DOWNTOWN HOSTEL MAP p.41, POCKET MAP B2. Vesturgata 17 📞 553 8120, 🌐 hostel.is. Vesturgata is a terrific spot – it's not only perfectly located for the harbour but is also an easy saunter to the bars, shops and restaurants around Austurstræti and Hafnarstræti. Swish and stylish, this HI place is actually more hotel than hostel, with six-berth dorms decorated in subtle pastel colours at unbeatable prices. **Dorm beds from 6550kr, double room 24,000kr**

Tjörnin and around

BALDURSBRÁ MAP p.47, POCKET MAP D7. Laufásvegur 41 📞 552 6646. Another of Reykjavík's long-standing accommodation options, this friendly, modern guesthouse enjoys a fantastic location, right in the city centre and overlooking Tjörnin. Though the price is good, rooms are a little cramped and the floral decor may not be to everyone's taste. The secluded garden with a hot tub for guests' use is, however, a definite boon and it's hard to find such a central location at this price. 18,000kr

HOLT MAP p.47, POCKET MAP E6. Bergstaðastræti 37 📞 552 5700, 🌐 holt .is. First opened in 1965, this is one of the most elegant and luxurious hotels in Reykjavík. With over three hundred paintings by Icelandic artists adorning the rooms and public areas, it's a little like staying overnight in an art gallery. Rooms are of the Persian-carpet, dark-wood-panelling, red-leather-armchair and chocolate-on-the-pillow variety. 54,000kr

RADISSON BLU SAGA REYKJAVÍK MAP p.47, POCKET MAP M2. Hagatorg 📞 525 9900, 🌐 radissonblu.com/sagahotel -reykjavik. This large, swanky business hotel is usually packed with conference delegates dashing up to admire the view from the top-floor restaurant. The rooms are cosmopolitan in feel and design, and feature bureaux and comfortable armchairs. Book early for the best rates. Bear in mind that it's a good thirty-minute walk from here to the shops and restaurants on Laugavegur. **30,000kr**

Bankastræti and around

FRÓN MAP p.54, POCKET MAP F5. Laugavegur 22A 🕿 511 4666, Ⓦ hotelfron.is. If you're self-catering, this hotel right in the city centre should be your first choice. In addition to regular double rooms, it offers stylish, modern studios (27,000kr) and larger apartments (28,800kr), each with bath, kitchenette and TV. Not only that, but the Bónus supermarket, offering the best prices on food and vegetables in town, is just across the road – perfect for when it comes to buying supplies. **27,000kr**

KLÖPP MAP p.54, POCKET MAP F4. Klapparstígur 26 🕿 595 8520, Ⓦ centerhotels.is. Despite its bizarre name, this is one of central Reykjavík's better hotels and a sound choice: modern throughout, with all rooms boasting tasteful wooden floors, oak furniture and wall panelling. Rooms can be a little on the small side, though, so it probably pays to ask to look at more than one if you're not happy with your allocation. The breakfast room is also a little cramped. **30,000kr**

REYKJAVÍK LOFT HOSTEL MAP p.54, POCKET MAP E4. Bankastræti 7 🕿 553 8140, Ⓦ hostel.is. The latest addition to the youth hostel scene in Reykjavík enjoys an unparalleled location right in the thick of things. There are six- to eight-bed dorms as well as private rooms. All rooms have private facilities and there's a top-floor café with balcony offering great views over the city centre. What's more, it's affiliated to HI, so there are discounts for members. **Dorms 8800kr, doubles 28,000kr**

ROOM WITH A VIEW MAP p.54, POCKET MAP F5. Laugavegur 18 🕿 552 7262,

Ⓦ roomwithaview.is. Quite simply, this place has got it right, offering a great selection of studios and apartments, all located on the sixth floor, overlooking the main shopping street, with incredible panoramic views from the shared balcony. Ten percent discount for stays of seven nights or more. **Budget studio 44,000kr, apartments 56,000kr**

SKJALDBREIÐ MAP p.54, POCKET MAP F5. Laugavegur 16 🕿 595 8510, Ⓦ centerhotels.is. This hotel is another of Reykjavík's long-standing hotel options and it's hard to beat on several counts. True, the plain rooms sporting classic Nordic decor may be rather uninspiring, but the price for such a central location is fairly competitive: bars, restaurants and shops are all right outside your window. Note, too, that the windows have extra sound-proofing – especially needed on raucous Friday and Saturday nights on Laugavegur. **58,000kr**

Hallgrímskirkja and around

ADAM MAP p.62, POCKET MAP F6. Skólavörðustígur 42 🕿 861 4142, Ⓦ adamhotel.com. Although this place likes to think it's a hotel, it's actually an upmarket guesthouse; the smart rooms all boast a kitchenette, though some share facilities. The location is also one of its best features, with Hallgrímskirkja as its next-door neighbour. **30,000kr**

FOSSHÓTEL BARON MAP p.62, POCKET MAP J5. Barónsstígur 2–4 🕿 562 3204, Ⓦ fosshotel.is. Another good choice if you're thinking of doing a bit of self-catering, as there are microwaves in most of the en-suite doubles and studios. Throughout, the decor is neutral and modern, if unsensational, and many rooms have sea views. The thirty-plus apartments vary greatly in size, so look before you choose. Discounts for stays of three nights and over. **Doubles 31,000kr, studios 44,000kr**

FOSSHÓTEL LIND MAP p.62, POCKET MAP K7. Rauðarárstígur 18 🕿 562 3350, Ⓦ fosshotel.is. Bright, modern and functional hotel offering discounts for stays of three nights or more, and worth considering if other more central places are fully booked. Rooms are plainly decorated and unadventurous, but the location's within easy reach of Hlemmur's buses which bring the city centre to within a brief bus ride, instead of a twenty- to thirty-minute walk. **37,000kr**

FOSSHÓTEL REYKJAVÍK MAP p.62, POCKET MAP P2. Þórunnartún 1 📞 531 9000, 🌐 fosshotel.is. Sprawling over sixteen floors, the *Fosshótel* chain's jewel in the crown opened for business in the summer of 2015 and is Iceland's biggest hotel, boasting 320 rooms, all with magnificent views over the city and the waterfront. Rooms are sleek and elegant, there's a spa and a gym, and even a pub with a great choice of beers. Be under no illusion, though – none of this comes cheap. **40,000kr**

GUESTHOUSE 101 MAP p.62, POCKET MAP K6. Laugavegur 101 📞 562 6101, 🌐 guesthouse101.is. What makes this guesthouse worth considering is its location – it's roughly a fifteen-minute walk along Laugavegur into the centre and on to Lækjartorg; or there's the Hlemmur bus interchange right outside the door for longer journeys or tired legs. Prices are also reasonable, but otherwise it's a rather soulless place with cheap furniture and cell-like rooms. **15,725kr**

HLEMMUR SQUARE MAP p.62, POCKET MAP K6. Laugavegur 105 📞 415 1600, 🌐 hlemmursquare.com. Upmarket dorm accommodation (dorms sleep from four to fourteen) is available on the upper floors of this stylish 1930s building located right beside Hlemmur. Facilities are shared, but linen and duvets are top-notch; no sleeping bags are allowed. There are also two kitchens on site for guest use. The top floor is given over to eighteen spacious and tastefully appointed double rooms. **Dorms 6000kr, doubles 37,000kr**

LEIFUR EIRÍKSSON MAP p.62, POCKET MAP G7. Skólavörðustígur 45 📞 562 0800, 🌐 hotelleifur.is. It's hard to imagine a hotel with such a perfect location – step outside the door and you're right in front of the Hallgrímskirkja, with all

Reykjavík has to offer a short stroll down Skólavörðustígur. It's a small, friendly and neatly furnished place to boot; the top-floor rooms, built into the sloping roof, are particularly worthwhile for their excellent views. **30,000kr**

LUNA MAP p.62, POCKET MAP F6. Spítalastígur 1 (Check in at Baldursgata 36) 📞 511 2800, 🌐 luna.is. If you're looking for spacious, beautifully decorated and superbly appointed apartments, this is the place to come. With modern and bright studios sleeping two people and larger apartments, also for two people, with high-quality fittings, this is a real home from home. There's also a three-room penthouse for rent. **Studios 25,000kr, apartments 35,900kr**

ÓÐINSVÉ MAP p.62, POCKET MAP F6. Þórsgata 1 📞 511 6200, 🌐 hotelodinsve.is. Long-established place that's stylish, relaxed and within an easy trot of virtually everything – Skólavörðustígur and Laugavegur, for example, are barely five minutes' walk away. The elegantly decorated rooms have wooden floors, neutral decor, comfortable Scandinavian-style furniture, and feature work by renowned Icelandic photographer, RAX. A pretty fair deal, especially given the way other hotels have raised their rates recently. **39,900kr**

REYKJAVIK4YOU APARTMENT HOTEL MAP p.62, POCKET MAP E5. Bergstaðastræti 12 📞 771 1200, 🌐 reykjavik4you.com. Not much to fault here: good-sized, comfortable and fully furnished modern apartments (with well-equipped kitchens) just moments from Laugarvegur, Hallgrímskirkja and the centre of town. It's typical of a new wave of accommodation springing up in response to the sudden boom in tourism since 2010, which is beginning to undermine (or complement) the more traditional high-end hotels. **42,000kr**

Öskjuhlíð and around

FOSSHOTEL RAUÐARÁ MAP p.67, POCKET MAP N3. Rauðarárstígur 37 📞 514 7000, 🌐 fosshotel.is. Though featuring widely on online booking sites – which can throw up some exceptionally good deals – this is a rather functional and uninspiring hotel, roughly twenty minutes' walk from the centre. The plain and simple rooms are clean and presentable, though you might find some disturbingly orange furnishings in them. Book in advance for the best rate quoted here. **29,000kr**

ICELANDAIR REYKJAVÍK NATURA MAP p.67, POCKET MAP N3. Nauthólsvegur 52 ☏ 444 4000, ⓦ icelandairhotels.com. A busy and impersonal hotel stuffed with stopover travellers (see box p.122). The 200-odd rooms here are nice enough, with wooden floors and comfortable modern furnishings throughout, though are on the small side. For some people, the location will be too far from the centre – it really is a bit of a trek into the centre, under subways and over bridges (30–40min), and in the evenings and at weekends buses here are rather infrequent. Free access to the hotel spa. **32,200kr**

SNORRI MAP p.67, POCKET MAP N3. Snorrabraut 61 ☏ 552 0598, ⓦ guesthousereykjavik.com. This pebble-dashed modern block is not one of Reykjavík's most alluring, and the rooms are rather uninspiring, too. But the location is a winner, just a short walk (10–15min) from the centre, and there's a choice of shared facilities or en-suite. The hotel is also on many of the city's bus routes, which means you will be able to get around quite easily should you base yourself here. **17,700kr**

Eastern Reykjavík

ARCTIC COMFORT MAP p.71, POCKET MAP Q3. Síðumúli 19 ☏ 588 5588, ⓦ arcticcomforthotel.is. Oddly located in a business district a good walk (30–40min) from the centre, it's worth considering this place only when everything else is full. Its out-of-town location is not great, but it is perfectly smart and clean and offers good value for money. Some rooms have self-catering facilities. There are several bus routes, too, which pass close by. **24,000kr**

CABIN MAP p.71, POCKET MAP P2. Borgartún 32 ☏ 511 6030, ⓦ hotelcabin .is. The best rooms in this good-value place are at the front, offering great views

out over the sea and Mount Esja. Warm autumn colours throughout, with lots of browns and greys making the decor pleasant and restful. The cheaper double rooms are only ten square metres in size and can feel a little cramped. Though it's a good twenty- to thirty-minute walk into the centre, there is a bus stop right outside the hotel. **22,500kr**

GRAND REYKJAVÍK MAP p.71, POCKET MAP P2. Sigtún 38 ☏ 514 8000, ⓦ grand.is. The clue's in the name: there's no shortage of opulence here, with marble floors, stylish chrome fittings and wood panels aplenty, though for the money you may wish to be closer to the centre – it's a 25-minute walk from here. Accommodation is in two buildings – the original and a newer, shimmering high-rise tower whose rooms enjoy stunning views. **43,200kr**

HILTON REYKJAVÍK NORDICA MAP p.71, POCKET MAP P3. Suðurlandsbraut 2 ☏ 444 5000, ⓦ reykjavik.nordica.hilton. com. The *Hilton* chain's one and only hotel in Iceland is big on Nordic minimalism: glass, chrome and natural wood are everywhere you look. Rooms at the front of the sprawling building enjoy views over the sea to Mount Esja. The hotel is popular with tour groups so it can feel rather anonymous given the number of guests here at any one time. **35,000kr**

ÍSLAND MAP p.71, POCKET MAP Q3. Ármúli 9 ☏ 595 7000, ⓦ hotelisland.is. Though it tends to change hands fairly frequently due to its out-of-town location, this is another of Reykjavík's long-standing and dependable accommodation options. Although a little too far from the centre to be your first choice (about 2.5km), the light and airy Scandinavian-designed rooms, with lots of wood panels, glass and chrome, make this worth considering if others are full. **28,600kr**

KRÍUNES MAP p.71, POCKET MAP R4. Vatnsendi, Kríunesvegi 12 ☏ 567 2245, ⓦ kriunes.is. With your own transport, it's worth considering this great little guesthouse located a fifteen-minute drive southeast of the city. A former farmhouse painted in warm Mediterranean colours and sporting lovely terracotta tiles and wooden floors, it certainly lives up to its name: sited beside the "end of the water", it enjoys a truly fantastic lakeside location, surrounded by high trees and with views of the water. 24,500kr

REYKJAVÍK CAMPSITE MAP p.71, POCKET MAP Q2. Sundlaugarvegur 32 ☎ 568 6944, Ⓦ reykjavikcampsite.is. This is the cheapest place to stay in Reykjavík, with cooking and shower facilities on site, plus some rather small two-berth cabins with bunk beds; facilities are shared. The site is perfectly located for Iceland's biggest and best swimming pool, Laugardalslaug. The city centre, though, is a good walk away (30–40min) so it might be worth considering taking the bus if you want to save your legs. Camping 2200kr, cabins 14,000kr

Hafnarfjörður and around

HAFNARFJÖRÐUR CAMPING MAP p.77. Hjallabraut 51 ☎ 565 0900, Ⓦ lavahostel.is/camping. Located within leafy Víðistaðatún park, off Flókagata north of the centre, the town's quiet campsite can make a nice alternative to the much bigger and busier site in Reykjavík. It's located in a quiet spot, has access to showers, and hot and cold running water, though for other facilities campers must use *Lava Hostel* next door. Mid-May to mid-Sept. 1700kr

HELGUHÚS MAP p.77. Lækjarkinn 8 ☎ 555 2842, Ⓦ helguhus.is. Named after the owner, Helga, this is one of the town's oldest accommodation options. It's a friendly, family-run guesthouse, and you'll be made to feel straight at home. There's just a handful of rather small and plainly decorated rooms which all share facilities, though there is access to a well-stocked kitchen should you choose to go self-catering. Note there's a three-night minimum stay. 43,700kr

HÓTEL VIKING MAP p.77. Strandgata 55 ☎ 565 1213, Ⓦ fjorukrain.is. If you're looking to get your Valhalla fix, this is the place to come. The 41 en-suite rooms bristle with over-the-top Viking decor, featuring lots of heavy wooden flourishes and gothic prints hanging on the walls. Next door to the main hotel there are

also fourteen new six-bed cabins. Guests have use of a sauna and hot tub. Doubles 24,000kr, cabins 33,000kr

LAVA HOSTEL MAP p.77. Hjallabraut 51 ☎ 565 0900, Ⓦ lavahostel.is. This hostel is one of Hafnarfjörður's best-value options and makes a sound choice if you're looking for somewhere cheaper than Reykjavík. It's housed in a handsome modern timber structure next to the campsite and offers compact dorms (sleeping 4–8) as well as regular double rooms. Both dorms and rooms share facilities and look out over the park. Dorms 5700kr, doubles 14,200kr

The Reykjanes Peninsula

NORTHERN LIGHT INN MAP p.81. 1 Northern Lights Road, off the Blue Lagoon approach road ☎ 426 8650, Ⓦ nli.is. This long building is half-hidden amid moss-covered lava flows, located just minutes from the Blue Lagoon. Rooms are plain but comfortable, there's a cosy lounge area with large fireplace, and the views from the restaurant are great. 37,950kr

STRANDARKIRKJA CAMPSITE MAP p.81. Strandarkirkja road, off Route 427. No phone. Spacious, grassy site close to the sea at this no-horse hamlet, run by a farmer who has installed showers, toilets, washing-up sinks and picnic tables. 1000kr

Golden Circle

IYHA DALSEL MAP p.88. Dalbraut 10, Laugarvatn, on Route 37 near the N1 roadhouse ☎ 899 5409, Ⓦ hostel. is. This newly refurbished hostel is conveniently located within a short walk of Fontana Spa, roughly halfway between the main Golden Circle sights of Þingvellir to the west, and Geysir and Gullfoss to the east. Dorms 5600kr, doubles 14,700kr

SKJÓL MAP p.88. On Route 35, halfway between Geysir and Gullfoss ☎ 899 4541, Ⓦ skjolcamping.com. Perfectly pitched between two of the country's most famous sights, there's a large campsite here, plus nine simple hostel-style rooms (all with shared facilities) with a separate restaurant/bar on hand. **Camping per person 1200kr, hostel beds 5000kr**

The south coast and Heimaey

ART HOSTEL MAP p.98. Hafnargata 9, Stokkseyri, above the old fish factory ☏ 854 4510, ⓦ arthostel.is. A much cosier, more comfortable place than you'd guess from the storm-battered exterior, with a range of well-furnished dorms and doubles – some with en-suites and kitchenettes. Good sea views. **Dorms 4500kr, doubles 14,000kr**

ÁSGARÐUR MAP p.98. Hvolstrod, Hvolsvöllur, off the Ringroad up Route 261, beside the church ☏ 487 1440, ⓦ asgardurinn.is. Tucked into a thin belt of woodland, there's a handful of comfortable cabins here which sleep up to four, each complete with self-contained bathroom and kitchen. Camping facilities also available. **14,500kr**

EDINBORG MAP p.98. Lambafell, Route 242 on the Seljavallalaug road ☏ 487 1212, ⓦ greatsouth.is. This tin-sided building contains a range of comfortable en-suite twins and family rooms; the clean lines and timber furnishings are smart but it's the surrounding wild scenery that is the real attraction. **27,500kr**

FRUMSKÓGAR GUESTHOUSE MAP p.98. Frumskógar 3, Hveragerði ☏ 896 2780, ⓦ frumskogar.is. Friendly, family-run guesthouse featuring small rooms with shared bathrooms and self-contained studio apartments, both with use of hot tubs and sauna. **23,500kr**

HAMRAGARÐAR CAMPSITE MAP p.98. Seljalandsfoss, 500m up Route 249 from the falls ☏ 866 7532 or ☏ 867 3535. Enjoying a wonderful setting with acres of thick grass for pitches, this site is just a short walk from the falls. There's also an indoor communal kitchen/dining room, plus a tiny bar, showers, toilets and laundry. **1300kr**

HEIMAEY CAMPSITE MAP p.98. 1km west of town at Herjólfsdalur ☏ 846 9111. This site enjoys a spectacular

location inside the collapsed bowl of an extinct volcano, with the grassy pitches half-encircled by high cliffs. **1300kr**

HOTEL SELFOSS MAP p.98. Eyravegi 2, Selfoss, close to the bridge ☏ 480 2500, ⓦ hotelselfoss.is. If you're after a "proper" multi-storey hotel with smart rooms and conference facilities, look no further than this dark block at the entrance to town. A good alternative to similar options in Reykjavík. **39,700kr**

HÓTEL SKÓGAFOSS MAP p.98. Skógar, on the falls road ☏ 487 8780, ⓦ hotelskogafoss.is. Long, single-storey building whose seventeen en-suite rooms are tidy and spacious, if a bit bland. Big breakfasts are available too, and you're just a short walk from the falls. **33,000kr**

HREIÐRIÐ MAP p.98. Corner of Faxastígur and Heiðarvegur ☏ 481 1045, ⓦ tourist .eyjar.is. The owner of this budget guesthouse has lived on Heimaey for decades and knows all the island's secret spots. Rooms are on the small side and facilities are shared. **12,500kr**

ICELANDAIR HOTEL MAP p.98. Route 1, Vík ☏ 487 1480, ⓦ icelandairhotels. com. This upmarket concrete-and-glass affair sports neatly furnished en-suite doubles with pine flooring and superb feature windows, some with sea views. **45,000kr**

IYHA SELFOSS MAP p.98. Austurvegur 28 (the Ringroad), Selfoss ☏ 482 1600, ⓦ hostel.is. Occupying a renovated old house close to the bus stop, this well-equipped hostel has slightly spartan dorms, a kitchen, small hot tub and handy café. **Dorms 5600kr**

IYHA SKÓGAR MAP p.98. Skógar, on the falls road ☏ 487 8801, ⓦ hostel. is. The bunk-bed dorms and doubles are pretty ordinary but good facilities include under-floor heating, a massive stainless-steel kitchen and a communal TV and dining area. **Dorms 5600kr, doubles 14,700kr**

IYHA VÍK MAP p.98. Suðurvíkurvegur 5, Vík, up near the church ☏ 487 1106, ⓦ hostel.is. This friendly, well-equipped hostel is very popular (in spite of its slightly stuffy dorms) and boasts a modern kitchen, plus a dining room with sea views. **Dorms 5600kr**

STRACTA MAP p.98. Rangárflatir 4, Hella, on the coastal side of Route 1 ☎ 531 8010, Ⓦ stractahotel.is. This large, modern, disorienting complex has corridors heading off in all directions. The rooms and apartments sport wooden floors, smart bathrooms and lots of white, with a clutch of on-site hot tubs and saunas. **30,000kr**

VATNSHOLT MAP p.98. Follow signposts 15km southeast of Selfoss via Route 305 ☎ 482 4829, Ⓦ hotelvatnsholt.is. Located on a farm, this large guesthouse offers a choice of accommodation spread between several buildings, with and without en-suite facilities. There's a plethora of pets too, including an arctic fox and a raven. **22,500kr**

VESTMANNAEYJAR HOTEL MAP p.98. Vestmannabraut 28 ☎ 481 2900, Ⓦ hotelvestmannaeyjar.is. A modern, welcoming venue whose spacious rooms feature polished wooden floors and leather lounges, with a hot tub for guests. **24,900kr**

ÞAKGIL MAP p.98. Turn inland 5km east of Vík at Höfðabrekka and follow the slow, twisting gravel Route 214 for 17km ☎ 893 4889, Ⓦ thakgil.is. Isolated valley with campsite and self-contained cabins with bunks sleeping up to four. There's also a communal dining area inside a large cave, and local hiking trails. June–Aug only. **Camping 1700kr, cabins 25,000kr**

The Interior

HIKING HUTS MAP p.105. Landmannalaugar, Laugarvegur and Þórsmörk Ⓦ fi.is and Ⓦ utivist.is. These huts are like giant communal chalets with large kitchens, toilets, showers and basic sleeping arrangements in bunks or on mattresses on the floor. Bring sleeping bags and food, and book ahead online – you can't just turn up. **Per person 8000kr**

LEIRUBAKKI MAP p.105. Route 26 ☎ 487 8700, Ⓦ leirubakki.is. This hotel and restaurant has Hekla's snow-smudged summit for a backdrop. Don't miss the outdoor lava-block "Viking Pool", which is tepid but affords great views of the mountain. The only downside is that it can get crowded with noisy tour groups. **Dorms 7200kr, doubles 31,000kr**

ESSENTIALS

Norðurgarði lighthouse, Reykjavík harbour

Arrival

You're most likely to arrive in Iceland at Keflavík International Airport, within a short bus ride of the capital, but there are a couple of other possibilities, depending on where you're coming from.

By air

Keflavík International Airport (KEF; S2; ⓦkefairport.is), Iceland's major arrivals hub, is 40km west of the capital via the multi-lane Route 41 expressway. It's a small, uncomplicated affair and you'll most likely be through passport control and in the arrivals hall within half an hour or so of landing; note that the duty-free shop is by far the cheapest place to buy spirits in Iceland. There are a number of ATMs in the arrivals lobby.

Taxis to the city wait outside the airport but it's a good idea to book ahead via ⓦairporttaxi.is; the journey to Reykjavík takes around 45 minutes and costs 16,000kr for a four-passenger vehicle during normal working hours – ask around the arrivals area to find people to share the fare.

Airport buses are far cheaper than taxis, meet flights and run direct to Reykjavík (45min). Reykjavík Excursions (ⓦre.is) and Gray Line (ⓦgrayline.is) sell tickets in the arrivals terminal and charge around 2500kr to their respective downtown terminuses, or 3000kr to your accommodation. Keflanding (ⓦkeflanding.com) is the cheapest option at 1900kr, but you need to book online and they run fewer services. For around 8500kr, you can also arrange airport–city transfers via the Blue Lagoon – a great introduction to Iceland, or a good final stop before leaving the country.

Reyjavík City Airport (RVK; ⓦisavia.is) is right on Reykjavík's southern outskirts and handles international flights from the Faroe Islands and Greenland, as well as domestic services from around the country. Catch Strætó bus #15 (440kr; 5min) or a taxi (1600kr; 5min) into the city.

By ferry

The **Norröna International Ferry** (ⓦsmyrilline.com) runs a Denmark–Faroes–Iceland route. This is worth considering if you want to bring your own vehicle to Iceland, though you land right across the country at Seyðisfjörður, 675km from Reykjavík. One-way fares from Denmark are €475 per person for one vehicle and two people sleeping in a couchette; a private cabin costs €680 per person. If you arrive by ferry but without your own vehicle, first catch a local bus to Egilsstaðir (45min; 1800kr) and then fly to Reykjavík (ⓦairiceland.is; online fare 14,000kr).

Getting around

Reykjavík's centre is so small that you can walk right across it in 30min, though city buses, bicycles and taxis come in handy for reaching some of the outlying sights and districts. For trips beyond the Greater Reykjavík area you'll need to make use of long-distance buses, car rental or tours – and, just possibly, a flight.

Stopovers

Icelandair (ⓦicelandair.com) will allow a stopover in Iceland for up to seven nights at no extra cost to your transatlantic ticket.

City bus

Stræto (w straeto.is) operate a network of numbered city buses, with the main terminus just east of the city centre at **Hlemmur Square**. Services run Mon–Fri 6.35am–midnight, Sat 7.30am–midnight and Sun 9.30am–midnight; English-language timetables can be downloaded from their website. Tickets cost 440kr a ride (pay on the bus, exact change only), with books of 20 tickets (8300kr) available on buses, or good-value one-day (1560kr) or three-day (3650kr) passes from newsagents around Hlemmur Square.

Taxi

Cabs are relatively inexpensive, and 1800–2200kr should get you across town; tipping is not expected. The main ranks are on Lækjargata; between Bankstræti and Amtmannsstígur; outside the Harpa concert hall; and in the vicinity of Hallgrímskirkja. For bookings, try Hreyfill (t 588 5522, w hreyfill.is) or BSR (t 561 0000, w bsr.is).

Bicycle

Reykjavík is comfortably scaled for riding a **bicycle** around, and you can also explore most of southern Iceland with a solid mountain bike or robust tourer. If you haven't brought your own along with you, bikes can be **rented** from some accommodation or from Reykjavík Bike Tours (w icelandbike.com), who also run a range of guided trips – expect to pay around 5000kr per day for a town bike, or 7250kr for something more sturdy. You should wear a helmet and weatherproof gear and, especially if you're venturing along some of the rougher roads outside the city, carry plenty of spares and a good-quality toolkit. In the countryside it's also wise to bring more than enough food and water, as it can be a very long way between shops and settlements. If it all gets too much, put your bike **on a bus** for 3800kr.

Long-distance bus

Long-distance buses cover much of the country, but not all year round. The most comprehensive coverage is provided by **Stræto** (w straeto.is), whose long-distance terminus is at Mjódd, 4km southeast of the city centre (catch bus #11 from the city terminus at Hlemmur); they run west to various locations on Reykjanes, as well as east along the Ringroad to Vík. Ringroad destinations are also covered by **Reykjavík Experience** (w re.is), based at the BSÍ bus station, 500m south of the centre of town at Vatnsmýrarvegi 10, who also run a bus to Geysir and Gullfoss; and **Sterna** (w sternatravel.com), whose main desk is at the Harpa Concert Hall (see p.42). For Interior destinations, **Trex** (w trex.is) operate daily from Reykjavík to Þórsmörk and Landmannalaugar, but only through the summer – roughly mid-June to early September.

Tickets for all these can be bought on the day, but it's best to book a couple of days in advance.

Weather and road conditions

Keep up to speed with English-language **weather forecasts** at w en.vedur.is, which gives appraisals for the week ahead. If you're travelling around outside of Reykjavík, check up-to-the-minute **road conditions** at w road.is, with online access to cameras and colour-coded maps.

Car

For a short trip to Iceland, a **car** gives you the flexibility you need for exploring outside the capital and will get you to many places not covered by buses. **Rental costs** are fairly competitive, especially if booked in advance or if you're visiting outside the June–September peak tourist season, when rates are lower. Companies either fix a daily maximum distance (say 100km) for the rental period, or allow unlimited mileage; **optional insurance** against windscreen damage, gravel damage, and how much of the **CDW** (Collision Damage Waiver) you'll be liable for, can double the daily rental cost. A general-purpose **two- or four-door**, capable of handling all the main roads and the better gravel tracks, will cost around 9500kr per day; a **camper van** will be at least 25,000kr a day (though you'll save on accommodation costs), while a **four-wheel-drive** – only advised if you have previous experience and want to reach Landmannalaugar or Þórsmörk under your own steam – costs upwards of 25,000kr. **Fuel** costs around 195kr per litre.

Vehicles are left-hand drives and you drive on the right. The speed limit is 50km/h in built-up areas, 90km/h on surfaced roads, and 80km/h on gravel. Seat belts are compulsory for all passengers, and headlights must be on at least half-beam all the time. **Road signs** include "Einbreið bru", indicating a single-lane bridge, and "Malbik endar", marking the end of a surfaced road. General warning signs are orange and marked "Varuð" or "Hætta" (warning or hazard).

Potential problems include having other vehicles spray you with windscreen-cracking gravel – so, when passing another car, slow down and pull over as far as possible, especially on unsurfaced roads. Outside the city, beware of the possibility of livestock wandering about. On gravel, or in snow and ice (unlikely during the summer), avoid skidding by keeping your speed down and applying the brakes slowly and as little as possible. In winter, rental vehicles are fitted with studded snow tyres, but you should carry food, water and a good blanket or sleeping bag in case your car gets stuck.

Flights

With the exception of the flight to Heimaey (see p.100), it's unlikely that you'll make use of Iceland's domestic airlines, Air Iceland (W airiceland. is) and Eagle Air (W eagleair.is) for transport. However, both also offer air tours over famous landscapes such as Hekla, Eyjafjallajökull, Þingvellir and Þórsmörk, lasting around 1hr 30min (€480) – check online for details.

Safe travel

If you're planning to hike, cycle or drive into Iceland's remoter corners, sign up first with W safetravel.is. The website provides alerts for hiking trail and highland road conditions, plus advice on how to prepare for your trip, and allows you to leave a travel plan and contact information with them, which will be followed up if you fail to report back at the appointed time.

In case of an emergency, **call 112**. For those with smartphones, there's also a free **112 app** available, which, when activated, transmits your location and nominated contact information to the rescue services.

Activities

Tours

Tours range from whale-watching cruises (see box, p.43) to hikes, pony treks (see p.126), cycle explorations of the city (see p.123), bus safaris and sightseeing flights (see p.124). Some, like the popular Golden Circle tour that takes in Þingvellir, Geysir and Gullfoss, you can do independently without too much bother, but in other cases you'll find that organized tours are the only practical way to reach an offbeat destination.

The widest range is offered between June and September. In the October–May low season, the roads to Landmannalaugar and Þórsmörk will be impassable and operators concentrate on Northern Lights, four-wheel- driving and glacier exploration along the fringes of the southern ice caps. **Booking in advance** is always advisable, whatever the time of year.

Swimming

Swimming is a major social activity in Iceland and almost every settlement has an outdoor swimming pool, geothermally heated to 28°C, along with hot pots (hot tubs) at 35–40°C, and a sauna or steam room. Out in the wilds, hot pots are replaced by natural hot springs, such as those at Landmannalaugar. Other than Laugardalslaug (see p.71), one of the most central pools in the city itself is the popular **Sundhöllin** at Barónsstígur 45A (☏ 411 5350, ⊕ itr .is; Mon–Thurs 6.30am–10pm, Fri 6.30am–8pm, Sat 8am–4pm, Sun 10am–6pm; 950kr; map p.62, pocket map H7), where there's a 25m indoor pool, two outdoor hot pots, plus single-sex nude sunbathing terraces. A new outdoor pool was added in 2017.

When using an Icelandic swimming pool, take off your shoes before entering the changing rooms and leave them in the rack provided; leave your towel in the shower area between the changing rooms and the pool, not in your locker (so you can dry off before returning to the changing rooms); and shower fully, with soap and without swimwear, before getting in the pool. Though there are always separate male and female changing rooms, very few pools have private cubicles.

Hiking

Southern Iceland is crossed by a web of **hiking trails**, the best known of which is the five-day Laugarvegur track between Landmannalaugar and Skógar via Þórsmörk (see box, p.107). But there are also plenty of much shorter hikes, lasting just a few hours, such as in the hills behind Hveragerði (see p.92) and various spots along the Reykjanes coast. Be aware, though, that even popular routes are seldom well marked; you'll always need to be competent at using navigational aids, especially in poor weather. It's also prudent to seek local advice about routes, though many make light of difficulties: a "straightforward" trail might involve traversing knife-edge ridges or dangerously loose scree slopes.

Always carry warm, weatherproof **clothing**, and wear tough hiking boots; being prepared means you can still get out and enjoy yourself in bad weather. You'll also need food and water, a torch, lighter, penknife, first-aid kit, a foil insulation blanket and a whistle or mirror for attracting attention; be sure to memorize Iceland's **emergency numbers** (see box, p.126). The prime hiking months are June through to August, when the weather is relatively warm, flowers are in bloom, and the wildlife is out and about – though even then you might experience snow inland.

Iceland has two main **hiking organizations**: Ferðafélag Íslands (Touring Club of Iceland; Mörkin 6, IS-108 Reykjavík, ☎568 2533, ⊛fi.is); and Útivist (Laugavegur 178, 105 Reykjavík, ☎562 1000, ⊛utivist.is). Contact them for general hiking information, group treks and to **book huts** at Landmannalaugar and Þórsmörk, and along Laugavegur.

Horseriding

Horses came to Iceland with the first Viking settlers, and have remained true to their original stocky Scandinavian breed. They're sturdy, even-tempered creatures and, in addition to the usual walk, trot, gallop and canter, can move smoothly across rough ground using the gliding *tölt* gait. Horses are available for hire from farms right across southern Iceland, but to organize something in advance, check out Íshestar (⊛ishestar.is) or Eldhestar (⊛eldhestar.is), which run treks lasting between an hour and several days for all experience levels.

Snow and action sports

There's not a huge enthusiasm for **skiing and snowboarding** in Iceland, perhaps because snow has generally been seen as just something you have to put up with. The main centre is around 20km from Reykjavík at **Bláfjöll** (⊛skidasvaedi.is), where there are a few short slopes and a ski lift, though this is only open through the winter months.

Surprisingly, one of the world's greatest freshwater **scuba dives** is at Silfra near Þingvellir, featuring ice-blue water with truly stunning visibility. You need to be already certified and, ideally, have dry-suit skills; contact Dive Iceland (⊛dive.is) or Dive Silfra (⊛divesilfra.is) for further details.

Directory A–Z

Addresses

Addresses in Iceland are given with the street name followed by the house number, post code and place i.e. "Hverfisgata 29, 101 Reykjavík".

Cinema

The multiplex Háskólabíó Cinema (Hagatorg, ☎591 5145, ⊛smarabio.is; map p.47, pocket map M3), attached to the university, is Reykjavík's main picture house. It screens mainstream film productions and is the only cinema in the country with Dolby Digital 3D.

Crime

Reykjavík is a relatively safe place with low levels of crime, most of it opportunistic: don't walk around the downtown area alone late at night, or leave valuables lying about or on show in a parked car, and you'll have few problems. The police (*lögreglan*) are English-speaking, unarmed and keen to help, should you need them; for general information dial ☎444 1000 or, in an **emergency**, ☎112.

Electricity

Electricity is 240v, 50Hz AC. Plugs and sockets are two-pin round prongs; make sure you carry an adaptor.

Embassies & consulates

Canada Túngata 14, 101 Reykjavík ☎575 6500, ⊛canadainternational. gc.ca; **China** Bríetartún 1, 105 Reykjavík

---

Emergency numbers

In an emergency, dial ☎112 for fire, ambulance or police.

☏527 6688, ⊚china-embassy.is;
Denmark Hverfisgata 29, 101 Reykjavík
☏575 0300, ⊚island.um.dk; **Finland**
Túngata 30, 101 Reykjavík ☏510 0100,
⊚finland.is; **France** Tungata 22, 101
Reykjavík ☏575 9600, ⊚ambafrance
.is; **Germany** Laufásvegur 31, 101
Reykjavík ☏530 1100, ⊚reykjavik.
diplo.de; **Greenland** Hverfisgata 29,
101 Reykjavík ☏575 0300, ⊚island
.um.dk; **Norway** Fjólugata 17, 101
Reykjavík ☏520 0700, ⊚noregur
.is; **Sweden** Lágmúli 7 ☏520 1230,
⊚swedenabroad.com; **UK** Laufásvegur
31, 101 Reykjavík ☏550 5100
⊚britishembassy.is; **USA** Laufásvegur
21, 101 Reykjavík ☏595 2200, ⊚is
.usembassy.gov.

Health

Reykjavík's health services are modern
and efficient, and all doctors will
speak English. No vaccinations are
required for visitors to Iceland. Water
is safe to drink everywhere.

In an **emergency**, dial ☏112 or get
to Landspitali Emergency Department,
Fossvogur, 108 Reykjavík (open 24hr;
pocket map N3). For less urgent
treatment, Reykjavík has fifteen
medical centres (*heilsugaeslan*);
your accommodation can contactone
for you, or there's a list available at
⊚heilsugaeslan.is/stadsetning. For
free treatment, Scandinavian citizens
must show medical insurance and a
valid passport, while citizens of the
European Economic Area need their
European Health Insurance Card and
passport. Otherwise you'll need to pay
at the time and then claim back the
money from travel insurance.

For **emergency dental treatment**
only, contact Tannlaeknavaktin at
Skipholt 33 (Mon–Fri 8am–10pm,
Sat & Sun 10am–8pm; ☏426 8000,
⊚tannlaeknavaktin.is), around
a twenty-minute walk east of
Hallgrímskirkja.

There are no 24hr **pharmacies**
(*apotek*) in Reykjavík, but one of the
longest-opening is Lyfja at Lágmúli 5,
108 Reykjavík (daily 8am–midnight;
☏533 2300). It's around 2km east of
Hallgrímskirkja.

Internet

Iceland is one of the highest per-
capita users of the internet. Most
Reykjavík cafés and accommodation
provide free wi-fi for customers, and
getting connected is seldom a problem
in the city.

Left luggage

If your accommodation can't store
luggage for you, there are lockers at
the BSÍ bus station, Vatnsmýrarvegi 10
(open 24hr; maximum three days); the
Reykjavík City Airport terminal (open
30min before first flight in the morning
and closes 30min after last arrival in
the evening; maximum thirty days); and
at Keflavík International Airport (daily
5am–5pm; maximum thirty days).

LGBT+ travellers

Given that Iceland is a fairly liberal
country – former prime minister
Jóhanna Sigurðardóttir was the
world's first openly lesbian head
of government – there's little
discrimination and, consequently, no
specifically gay venues in Reykjavík.
For listings check out ⊚gayice.is, or
for general information contact the
Icelandic LGBT+ association, Samtökin
78 (Suðurgata 3, Reykjavík ☏552
7878, ⊚samtokin78.is).

Money

Icelandic krónur (Isk, Ikr or kr) come
in 5000kr, 2000kr, 1000kr and 500kr
notes, with 100kr, 50kr, 10kr, 5kr
and 1kr coins. There are plenty of
banks with ATMs in central Reykjavík
and larger towns; you can also find

ATMs at some country fuel stations. However, you can pay for almost anything in Iceland using bank debit or credit cards (Visa and Mastercard are the most widely accepted), and it's quite feasible to spend a week here without using cash – except on Stræto buses (see p.123).

Opening hours

Generally, business hours are Monday to Friday 10am–6pm and Saturday 10am until mid-afternoon; if they open on Sunday, it will probably be after noon. In Reykjavík and larger towns, supermarkets open daily from 10am until late afternoon; in smaller communities, however, some places don't open at all at weekends. Country fuel stations provide some services for travellers, and larger ones tend to open daily 9am–10pm. Office hours are Monday to Friday 9am–5pm.

Phones

Icelandic phone numbers are seven digits long, with no area codes. Phone directories are ordered by Christian name – Jakob Gunnarsson, for example, would be listed under J, not G. Landline rates are cheapest for domestic calls at weekends and 7pm–8am Monday–Friday; on calls to Europe daily 7pm–8am; and to everywhere else daily 11pm–8am.

Iceland uses both GSM and NMT (Nordic Mobile Telephone) mobile phone networks. GSM covers Reykjavík and almost all the surrounding region; coming from the UK or EU, your own country's pay-as-you-go SIM cards might work with varying roaming rates, or buy a new pay-as-you-go SIM from fuel stations or newsagents in Iceland. You'll only need NMT coverage for remoter interior regions; contact Icelandic car rental companies or hiking organizations (see p.125) for more information.

Post

Post offices are open Monday to Friday 9am–4.30pm, though a few in Reykjavík have longer hours. Domestic mail takes around two working days; count on three to five days for mail to reach the UK or US, and a week to ten days to reach Australia and New Zealand. Anything up to 50g costs 153kr within Iceland, 180kr to Europe, and 240kr to anywhere else; up to 100g costs 185/310/490kr. For parcel rates, check ⓦpostur.is.

Safety

You need to be responsible for your own safety in Iceland; there are so many natural hazards that it is impossible to fence them all off, and you shouldn't expect to find warning signs, safety barriers or guide ropes even at extremely dangerous locations, such as the edge of waterfalls, volcanoes or boiling mud pits.

The summer sun is strong, especially when reflected off ice or snow, so use sunscreen and wear sunglasses. Moisturizer and lip balm help protect against cold dry air, wind and dust.

Hypothermia – when your core body temperature drops dangerously – occurs if you get simultaneously exhausted, wet and cold; symptoms include a weak pulse, disorientation, numbness and slurred speech. Treatment involves getting as dry and as warm as possible, and taking sugary drinks – though not alcohol. Serious cases need hospital treatment. Avoid hypothermia by eating sufficient carbohydrates, drinking plenty of water and wearing warm and weatherproof clothing.

Smoking

Smoking is banned indoors in public buildings, restaurants, bars and cafés, and on school grounds, sport facilities or public areas of apartment buildings. Smoking is also prohibited inside most accommodation. You need to be at least 18 years old to purchase cigarettes, which are only sold by convenience stores and a few bars.

Tax refunds

If you spend more than 6000kr in any single transaction on goods to take out of the country, you are entitled to a tax refund of fifteen percent of the total price, as long as you leave Iceland within ninety days. Ask for a **Refund Tax Free form** when you make your purchases, which needs to be filled out by the shop. Money can be refunded in full back onto your credit/debit card at refund points located in the departure halls at Keflavík and Reykjavík airports; on board all international cruise ships two hours before departure; or at Reykjavík port's Visitor Centre. The same places, plus refund points at Kringlan Shopping Mall and Reykjavík's Tourist Information centres (see below), can make the refund in cash, but this incurs a commission.

Time

Iceland is on Greenwich Mean Time (GMT) year-round. GMT is five hours ahead of US Eastern Standard Time and ten hours behind Australian Eastern Standard Time.

Tipping

Tipping is not expected anywhere in Iceland, including for service in hotels, restaurants and taxis.

Tourist information

The **Reykjavík Tourist Office** is in the heart of the old town (at Aðalstræti 2; June to mid-Sept daily 8.30am–7pm; mid-Sept to May Mon–Fri 9am–6pm, Sat 9am–4pm, Sun 9am–2pm; ☏ 590 1550, ⊚ visitreykjavik.is). They're a useful source of information for local events, and can also help organize or advise about tours, accommodation and car rental. It's also worth checking out **Reykjavík Grapevine** (⊚ grapevine.is), an irreverent weekly listings magazine which reviews attractions, parties, bands, restaurants and upcoming events.

Travellers with disabilities

Icelandic hotels are required by law to make a percentage of their rooms accessible. Transport – including ferries, airlines and some tour buses – can make provisions for wheelchair users if notified in advance.

Reykjavík's Disabled Association, Sjálfsbjörg, is at Hátún 12, 105 Reykjavík (☏ 550 0360, ⊚ sjalfsbjorg .is, ⊚ sjalfsbjorg@sjalfsbjorg.is), and can advise on accessible accommodation and travel around Iceland.

Travelling with children

Reykjavík's supermarkets and pharmacies are well stocked with nappies and formula (though keep in mind where the next shops might be in the countryside). In bad weather, swimming pools – some of which have waterslides – make great places for children to let off steam. Be aware that special care needs to be taken at outdoor sites (see opposite).

Festivals and events

Though Iceland's calendar is essentially Christian, many official holidays and festivals have a secular theme.

Þorrablót

February

A midwinter feast once honouring the Viking weather god Þorri. People eat traditional foods such as *svið* (sheep's head) and *hákarl* (fermented shark).

Bjórdagur (Beer Day)

March 1

Festival honouring the date in 1989 that Iceland's 74-year-old prohibition on beer was lifted. Best experienced by joining in a *rúntur* (bar crawl).

Sjomannadagur (Seamen's Day)

June 4

Expect mock sea-rescue demonstrations, swimming races and tug-of-war battles, especially around Reykjavík's old harbour.

Independence Day

June 17

The day the Icelandic state separated from Denmark in 1944. Low-key events held in central Reykjavík.

Jónsmessa

June 24

Magical creatures are said to be out in force, playing tricks on the unwary. Some people celebrate with a big bonfire; others roll around naked in the morning dew.

Verslunnarmannahelgi (Labour Day Weekend)

First weekend in August

Traditionally, everybody heads into the countryside, sets up camp, and parties themselves into oblivion.

Þjóðhátíð

First weekend in August

Held inside an extinct volcano crater on Heimaey (see p.100), and celebrated in much the same spirit as Labour Day on the mainland. Book transport and accommodation a year in advance.

Rettir

Autumn

The *rettir*, or stock round-up, takes place in rural areas throughout September. Horses and sheep are herded from the higher summer pastures to be penned; some farms allow visitors to watch or even participate.

Public holiday dates

Jan 1 New Year's Day

March/April Maundy Thursday, Good Friday, Easter Sunday, Easter Monday

April, first Thursday after April 18 First day of summer

May 1 May Day

May/June Ascension Day, Whit Sunday, Whit Monday

June 17 National Day

August Bank Holiday (first Monday)

Dec 24–26 Christmas Eve, Christmas Day, Boxing Day

Dec 31 New Year's Eve

Chronology

16 million years ago As the Eurasian and North American tectonic plates begin to tear apart, Iceland first pops out of the waves during volcanic eruptions.

300 BC Historian Pytheas of Marseille writes about a frozen Arctic land named "Ultima Thule", possibly Iceland.

c.800 AD Christian monks from Ireland settle the southern coast.

c.850 A Viking adventurer named Naddoddur accidentally discovers Iceland.

874 Norwegian-born Ingólfur Arnarson settles the area of Reykjavík ("Smoky Bay"), becoming the country's first known resident.

870–930 Vikings, mostly from Norway, colonize all Iceland during the Landnám, or Settlement Period.

930 Iceland declares itself a Commonwealth, with an annual parliament held at Þingvellir.

980–1000 Vikings discover Greenland and North America.

1000 Christianity becomes Iceland's national religion.

1104 Hekla erupts violently, burying farms across the south of the country.

1220–62 The "Sturlung Age" ushers in a period of civil war; many of Iceland's historic sagas are written down, extolling the virtues of earlier times.

1262 The "Old Treaty" cedes Icelandic sovereignty to Norway, ending the civil war.

1280 The *Jónsbók* of laws is compiled.

1397 The Kalmar Union sees Norway, and hence Iceland, brought under Danish rule.

1402 Plague arrives in Iceland; almost half the population dies.

1420–1532 Denmark, England and Germany tussle over Icelandic trading rights during the "English Century".

1550 As the Reformation sweeps Europe, Iceland's last Catholic bishop, Jón Arason, is executed at Skálholt and the country becomes Lutheran.

1602 Denmark imposes a repressive trade monopoly on Iceland, beggaring the country and reducing the population to the status of tenant farmers.

1752 Bailif Skúli Magnússon founds an Icelandic trading company, whose warehouses at Reykjavík become the core of Iceland's first town.

1783 Poisonous fallout from the gigantic Lakí eruptions in eastern Iceland sterilizes farms across the country, causing famines and killing a third of the population.

1787 Denmark lifts the trade monopoly.

1835 Jónas Hallgrímsson (and later Jón Sigurðsson) champions the idea of Icelandic nationalism and independence from Denmark.

1843 The Danish king approves reconstitution of the Alþing at Reykjavík.

1871 Denmark annexes Iceland.

1904 Home Rule: Denmark grants political independence to Iceland.

1918 Iceland becomes an independent Danish state.

1940-45 During World War II, British and US forces occupy Iceland. After Denmark is captured by the Nazis, Iceland declares itself fully independent on June 17, 1944.

1949–51 As the Cold War gains momentum, Iceland joins NATO and the US opens an airbase at Keflavík.

1958–85 Iceland gradually expands its territorial waters to a two-hundred-mile (320km) radius around the country, sparking a series of "Cod Wars" with Britain over fishing rights.

1994 Iceland becomes part of Europe, but stops short of joining the EU.

1998–2008 Unregulated attempts to diversify the economy away from fishing by investing in banking creates a financial bubble which implodes in 2008, leaving twenty percent of Icelanders bankrupt.

2010 The Eyjafjallajökull volcano erupts in a mighty ash cloud, causing aviation chaos in Europe – and bringing Iceland's raw landscape to the attention of international tourism.

2011–2018 Tourist numbers grow twenty percent annually, reaching nearly two million visitors in 2018 – compared with a national population of just 331,000. Tourism becomes the biggest single source of revenue.

Language

Icelandic is a medieval language, retaining much of the complex grammar that has largely dropped out of use elsewhere in Europe. And while you might even recognize a few dialect nouns – tjörn for tarn (small pond), fjall for fell (mountain) – the pronunciation will leave you reeling (fjall is pronounced "fyatl", for example). Fortunately most Icelanders speak **English**, alongside other Nordic languages and a smattering of French and German; as they don't expect foreigners to know a word of Icelandic you'll delight everyone by attempting even the simplest phrase.

There are **32 letters** in the Icelandic alphabet, including Þ (þ) and Ð (ð) – both, to all intents and purposes, pronounced "th". Bizarrely, there is no exact Icelandic equivalent for the word "interesting" – the closest being *gaman*, fun.

An idea of pronunciation is given in brackets where useful.

BASIC WORDS AND PHRASES

I don't understand	ég skil ekki (yairg skil ekee)
Could you speak more slowly?	gætirðu talað hægar? (gye-tiroo talath hyegar)
Do you speak English?	talarðu ensku? (talarthoo enskoo)
Yes	já (yau)
No	nei (nay)
Hello	hæ (hi)
Good morning/afternoon	góðan dag (go-than dargh)
Good night	góða nótt (go-tha not)
Goodbye	bless
Please	afsakið (afsakith)
Thank you	takk fyrir
What's your name?	hvað heitirðu? (kvath haytiroo?)
I'd like...	ég ætla að fá (yairg aytla ath fau)
Excuse me	fyrirgefðu (fyrir gef thoo)
How much does it cost?	hvað kostar þetta? (kvath kostar thetta?)
Where	hvar (kvar)
Toilet	snyrting
Men/women	karlmenn/kvenmenn
Open/closed	opið/lokað (opith/lokath)
Bill/check, please	reikninginn, takk

FOOD AND DRINK

arctic char	bleikja
beer	bjór
bread	brauð
burger	hamborgari
butter	smjör
cheese	ostur
cod	þorskur
coffee	kaffi
egg	egg
fermented shark	hákarl
fish	fiskur
herring	síld
hot dog	pylsur
Icelandic vodka	brennivín
Icelandic yoghurt	skyr
lamb	lamb
lobster	humar
milk	mjólk
pancakes, flatbread	laufabrauð, flatbrauð
pepper	pipar
pizza	pítsa
ptarmigan	rjúpa
reindeer	hreindýr
salmon	lax
salt	salt
skimmed milk	lettmjólk
smoked lamb	hangikjöt
soup	súpa
"steam bread"	hverabrauð
sugar	sykur
tea	te
trout	silungur
water	vatn
wind-dried cod	harðfiskur

Publishing information

This second edition published June 2018 by **Rough Guides Ltd**
Distribution
UK, Ireland and Europe
Apa Publications (UK) Ltd; sales@roughguides.com
United States and Canada
Ingram Publisher Services; ips@ingramcontent.com
Australia and New Zealand
Woodslane; info@woodslane.com.au
Southeast Asia
Apa Publications (SN) Pte; sales@roughguides.com
Worldwide
Apa Publications (UK) Ltd; sales@roughguides.com
Special sales, content licensing and co-publishing
Rough Guides can be purchased in bulk quantities at discounted prices. We can create special editions, personalized jackets and corporate imprints tailored to your needs. sales@roughguides.com
roughguides.com
Printed in China
All rights reserved
© 2018 Apa Digital AG and Rough Guides Ltd
No part of this book may be reproduced in any form without permission from the publisher except for the quotation of brief passages in reviews.
140pp includes index
A catalogue record for this book is available from the British Library
ISBN 978-0-24130-651-2
The publishers and authors have done their best to ensure the accuracy and currency of all the information in **Pocket Rough Guide Reykjavík**, however, they can accept no responsibility for any loss, injury, or inconvenience sustained by any traveller as a result of information or advice contained in the guide.

Rough Guides credits

Editor: Keith Drew, Rebecca Hallett
Layout: Pradeep Thapliyal
Cartography: Ed Wright
Picture editor: Michelle Bhatia

Photographer: Diana Jarvis
Managing editor: Keith Drew
Cover photo research: Marta Bescos
Senior DTP coordinator: Dan May

Author:

David Leffman was born and raised in the UK, spent twenty years in Australia, then relocated back to Britain in 2009. Since 1992 he has authored and co-authored guides to Australia, China, Indonesia, Iceland and Hong Kong for Rough Guides, Dorling Kindersley and others, ghostwritten a Chinese cookbook and contributed articles for various publications on subjects ranging from crime to martial arts and history. If he had spare time he'd go scuba diving.

Help us update

We've gone to a lot of effort to ensure that the first edition of the **Pocket Rough Guide Reykjavík** is accurate and up-to-date. However, things change – places get "discovered", opening hours are notoriously fickle, restaurants and rooms raise prices or lower standards. If you feel we've got it wrong or left something out, we'd like to know, and if you can remember the address, the price, the hours, the phone number, so much the better.

Please send your comments with the subject line "**Pocket Rough Guide Reykjavík Update**" to mail@roughguides.com. We'll credit all contributions and send a copy of the next edition (or any other Rough Guide if you prefer) for the very best emails.

Photo credits

All photos © Rough Guides except the following:
(Key: t-top; c-centre; b-bottom; l-left; r-right)

Cover Leifur Eiríksson Statue and Hallgrímskirkja Getty Images

p1 iStock
p2 Shutterstock (t); Alamy (bl & br)
p4 Getty Images
p5 Getty Images
p6 Getty Images
p10 Shutterstock
p11 Shutterstock (t & b)
p12 Shutterstock (t)
p13 Shutterstock (c); Alamy (cr)
p14 Shutterstock (t & b)
p15 Shutterstock (b)
p16 Shutterstock (t); AWL Images / John Warburton-Lee (b)
p17 Getty Images (b)
p20 Shutterstock (t, c, b)
p21 Karl Petersson (b)
p22 Shutterstock (t & c); iStock (b)
p23 Shutterstock (t & b); iStock (c)
p33 Superstock (t)
p36 Getty Images
p37 Superstock (t)
p48 Alamy
p49 Alamy
p50 Karl Petersson
p59 Mikael Axelsson
p60 iStock
p63 Shutterstock
p69 Reykjavík Art Museum / Vigfús Birgisson
p72 Shutterstock
p73 Getty Images
p76 Alamy
p77 James MacDonald
p90 Shutterstock (t)
p91 Alamy (t)
p93 Shutterstock (t)
p95 www.arctic-images.com
p96 Shutterstock
p97 Shutterstock
p98 Shutterstock
p99 Shutterstock
p100 Alamy
p104 Shutterstock
p107 Shutterstock
p108 Alamy (t & b)
p109 Dreamstime / Neverse
pp110–111 Alamy
pp120–121 Shutterstock

SMALL PRINT

Index

Maps are marked in **bold**.

Long bus journey?
Phone run out of juice?

1 Denim, the pencil, the stethoscope and the hot-air balloon were all invented in which country?

a. Italy　　　　　c. Germany
b. France　　　　d. Switzerland

2 What is the busiest airport in the world?

a. London Heathrow　　c. Chicago O'Hare
b. Tokyo International　　d. Hartsfield-Jackson
　　　　　　　　　　　　　Atlanta International

3 Which of these countries does not have the equator running through it?

a. Brazil　　　　b. Tanzania
c. Indonesia　　d. Colombia

4 What is the principal religion of Japan?

a. Confucianism　　c. Jainism
b. Buddhism　　　　d. Shinto

5 Every July in Sonkajärvi, central Finland, contestants gather for the World Championships of which sport?

a. Zorbing　　　　　c. Chess-boxing
b. Wife-carrying　　d. Extreme ironing

6 What colour are post boxes in Germany?

a. Red　　　　c. Blue
b. Green　　　d. Yellow

7 For three days each April during Songkran festival in Thailand, people take to the streets to throw what at each other?

a. Water　　　　c. Tomatoes
b. Oranges　　　d. Underwear